I0037315

G.I. WEALTH MANUAL

— A PRACTICAL GUIDE —

TO GETTING YOUR ACTIVE DUTY FINANCIAL SH*T IN ORDER & FULLY RETIRE AT 20-YEARS

IAN R. BERGSTROM

GI WEALTH MANUAL

A Practical Guide to Getting your Active Duty Financial Sh*t in Order and Fully Retire at 20-Years

Copyright Ó 2022. Ian Bergstrom. All Rights Reserved. No part of this publication may be reproduced, distributed, or transmitted in any form or by any means, including photocopying, recording, or other electronic or mechanical methods, without the prior written permission of the publisher, except in the case of brief quotations embodied in critical reviews and certain other noncommercial uses permitted by copyright law.

ISBN: 979-8-218-05013-9

Transcendent Publishing
PO Box 66202
St. Pete Beach, FL 33736
www.TranscendentPublishing.com

Printed in the United States of America.

Disclaimer: The ideas, concepts, and everything else in this book are completely opinion-based on what has worked for me in my wealth creation ventures. It may not work for you, and it may not continue to work for me in the long run as taxes, regulations, and markets change.

This book is for educational and entertainment purposes. I am not a tax or certified financial professional. This book was written from my and others' experiences and positive habits and actions. Please consult with a tax professional and/or a certified financial professional before acting upon ideas in this book.

I make no representations as to the accuracy, completeness, currency, and validity of the information in this book. I will not be held liable for any errors or omissions in the information that could result in any losses, injuries, or damages from its use. All actions are solely your responsibility as there are absolutely no guarantees! Ian Bergstrom, giwealthmanual.com, and Mountain Stream Ventures LLC are not registered or licensed as investment advisors with the SEC. Ian Bergstrom, giwealthmanual.com, and Mountain Stream Ventures LLC do not offer personalized investment advice. Only your registered/licensed financial advisor can give you personalized investment advice.

This book has no connection or endorsement by the US Department of Defense or any other US Government Agency.

"The best investment you can make is an investment in yourself...the more you learn, the more you'll earn."

– Warren Buffett

Table of Contents

Introduction

Before I begin, I want to thank you for your service. And if you picked up this book and happen to not be in the military, I thank you for taking steps to secure your own financial future. Not, because it is my book, but because you can improve your life and your subordinate's lives by guiding them...and that is my mission, to improve the wealth of the US fighting force. While this book is going to be focused mainly on how military members can leverage the advantages that come with the career, anyone can take the financial principles outlined in this book and gain control of their finances and excel at them.

My vision for this book is to be a practical guide broken down by ranks and milestones you should be looking to achieve. I will also be dedicating some chapters to a topic that affects all ranks and is paramount for good financial literacy. I will be fully transparent with my mistakes and wins, so hopefully, you'll get a good idea of where to head. This path worked well for me, and I hope it does for you too! There's very little fluff included within these pages, with actionable steps that you can take to get from where you are starting to your own financial goals. And if you have no current financial goals, then I will help you with those as well.

For those that are planning on serving a full 20 years, I ultimately want to provide you with the financial knowhow on how to grow your finances and track record enough that you could easily fully retire at the end of those 20 years... yes, not having to work another day after retirement, if you choose not to. But...I can't make that a promise just because you bought this book. It is ultimately your promise to yourself; you must learn from this book, apply, and master the technique outlined. You won't accomplish that by just holding this book, and I won't be there to hold your hand. So, get after it, and you will achieve it! But you've taken a great first step to learning how!

Now, why the hell do I have the credentials to be speaking on this matter? Great question! I should probably take the time to tell you who I am. My name is Ian Bergstrom. I was born and raised in Podunk, Ohio. I was taught to go to school, get good grades, and told that a job will grace me with the financial support to live a long and happy life...so that is what I began to do. I assume that is what many of you heard as well. I sought after good grades in high school, which earned me a spot in a great college (THE Ohio State University. Michiganders, just close the book now...just joking, you can remain), and decided to commission through ROTC with the vision of leveraging my Meteorology degree and the hope of traveling the world.

Don't get me wrong, I accomplished all that, but I felt that there was something more to life than this. I was in control of my personal life...as much as I could in the military. But I realized I was just following the Baby Boomer mindset that my parents instilled, which does not necessarily apply anymore to our Gen X and Z future. A job does not secure our future; we must secure our own! I set off on a journey to learn how to do that for myself, and that is what I would like to carry forward through this book—to help my brothers and sisters in arms secure their futures! I may not have the title of a Financial Planner, Advisor, or any other fancy title (besides MBA, meh). But I do have quite a bit of first-hand experience, acquired knowledge, and plenty of mistakes that makes me a strong ally in this department. Because before, I did it poorly. So, learn from me. I was super passionate and interested in personal finance and I would listen to every Jack and Jill that would tell me to do something "financially savvy." *Well, there's your problem, Ian.* I bounced from stocks to real estate, to fancy life insurance policies (a rip-off, in my opinion), mutual funds, gold and silver, etc. And I will admit... I even got wrapped up in one of those MLM schemes...I know, I was that guy! The list goes on and on. Did it help me reach new levels of wealth!? Hell no. I bounced around so often that I lost more money than I made. I thought I was doing great as a six-year O-3 with a net worth of $100K... until I talked to my friend in the same year group who had just pumped all their money into a mutual fund, had a roommate, and a net worth of $500K already...yes, half a million! I was shocked, disgusted, and motivated to do better.

The thing I did learn through is what I did and didn't enjoy doing in the investment world. I hated dealing with the emotion of tenants, lugging physical silver and gold around, life insurance policies, and mutual funds. (I'll explain this later.) It also forced me to focus on who I need to listen to and who I should tell to go pound sand. So...I concentrated, focused, and got serious in two areas: my personal day-to-day finances and stock investing. I believe this is where most should concentrate in their journey, as it is easy as shit to get started, works with your budget, and is simple to understand. It is so simple—it's what led me to write this book, to help other military members cut through the noise. Now, if you are interested in these other areas of investment, I will do my best to provide a list of solid books and resources to help you explore those areas to see if they are right for you!

I have worked with some strong mentors in my military career that are prominent in the personal finance sector (even dropping upwards of $60K to be a part of their inner circles), which has allowed me to move from a net worth of less than $10K to one that is pushing $250K just three years later, and growing exponentially ever since. So, to prevent you from shelling out that hard-earned cash on less than savory investments and to avoid my pitfalls, I want to help guide you forward with this book.

Sub-disclaimer...I was in the military, and you, the reader, are most likely in the military or on your way...I am not going to sugarcoat my language, so be prepared. Buckle your Kevlar, get cozy in your woobie, and have your packets of Jalapeño Cheese ready, because here we go on a journey to secure your financial future.

MOVE OUT!

CHAPTER 1

Removing Piss Poor Mindset

Say it with me, everyone! *"Go to college, work for a great company, and retire at 60!"*

This is the exact bullshit mindset we need to strip—amongst many others that we learned from our Baby Boomer parents! This worked amazingly well when college tuition was payable by a minimum wage job and most jobs out of college were offering a pension for the rest of your life if you gave them 20+ years. This is not the case anymore…even with the military and removal of the guaranteed pension (but we will get into this later). I call this the Baby Boomer mindset and will refer to it as such going forward.

Go to College

Let's break this Baby Boomer mindset down. First, we arrive at *"Go to College."* I am going to say that this is the most bullshit of them all. Not everyone needs to and should go to college, and this isn't an intellectual thing (although in some cases, it is). College is set to train you in a specialized field (Doctor,

Engineer, Scientist, Teacher, etc.). You do not need to be specialized in Liberal Arts or Underwater Basket Weaving. And this is just coming from the return on investment (ROI) of the degree—the amount of debt that you acquire from going to college these days does not math out to the career that the average person receives after.

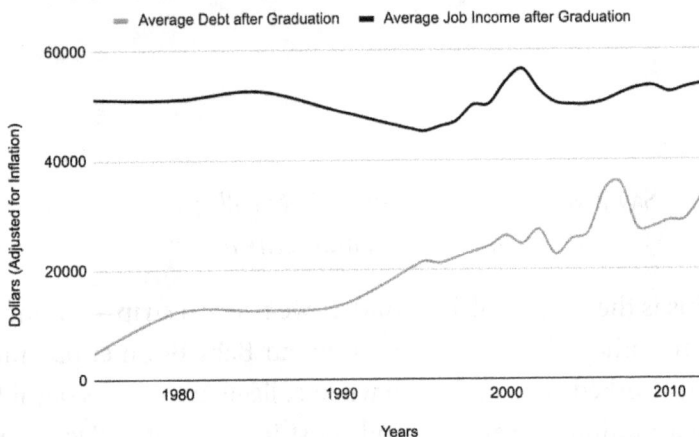

Figure 1 – Comparison of the Average Debt held by College Students post-graduation[1] and the Average Reported Entry-Level Income post-graduation[2]

College tuition and room/board have climbed consistently since 1973, while entry-level incomes for recent graduates have remained relatively constant. Not a good thing—enjoy your debt and the many years it takes to pay it off.

What is so special about 1973, you may ask? This doesn't really help with your financial literacy, but it does provide some solid trivia knowledge and some additional understanding.

1973 is when the Pell Grant was introduced by the Federal Government to colleges and students. Woo-hoo, this sounds like a great thing on the surface, but like most government handouts, it's not so great underneath. I am trying not to get political here, but it is just the fact of the matter. We have seen this with Medicare/Medicaid, and rising healthcare costs, and we have seen it with education. When the government offers "free," risk-free, guaranteed money to universities, the greedy side of us human beings will kick in and continually ask for more and more money. If it is continually given, then that cost of attendance will keep getting higher and higher. Higher salaries and cost of living do cause these tuition costs to rise as well. In the end, to lower these costs, measures need to be made in order to remove "guaranteed" money from the system, and to get the government out of educational financing.

So, be thankful that if you didn't go to college, you didn't incur these crazy debt loads. And for you officers that did go to college, hopefully you received a scholarship because they are not 100% guaranteed if you went the ROTC route. And if you did get hit with one of these loans, we will talk about repayment strategies in the coming chapters. Pst...I was one in the ROTC position that did not get a scholarship...so it does happen.

The military is a legit college alternative. So, congrats on making a great personal, financial, professional, and educational decision for your future. There are so many perks that come with the military (mainly positive, but some negative). Another great choice for those who do not have a specialization in mind would be a trade school (so many needed professions coming out of these schools as of 2021— they pay very, very well for the talents earned). And the other and most financially sound option is going into business for yourself (how most fortunes are made).

Get a Good Job

The second part of the lovely Boomer Mindset is *"Get a Good Job."* I find this one funny because they never specify what a "good" job is. And "good" is different for everyone. So, this part is not "wrong" per se; it just is shitty verbiage.

Let's make it better. Instead of being very vague in the language, let's specify what is "good." How about "Get a job that supports your desired lifestyle and goals?" My main goal was to continue in Meteorology and travel the world, the Air Force fit that goal for me. And at 10 years in, the military stopped fulfilling that goal, and it was time to buck up and find a new job that furthered my goals.

Everyone has a different desired lifestyle that they currently want to maintain, and what they would like to maintain in the future. And when I say "job," I just mean source of income. So, it could be anything if it funds your passions, your ability to live, and supports you. Then that is your "job." "Goals," are another critical facet. There is a wise adage that goes:

> *"In order to know where you want to go, you must first know where you are currently at and define where you want to be."*

Remove the fancy talk—set the primary goal (destination), know your current situation, and define milestones to get you to your destination (subgoals). But we will get into goal setting a little later because it is a massive factor determining financial health and wealth.

Retire at 60

This part of the poor mindset hasn't changed much. Most people will retire by the age of 60, which is fine and dandy... if it is your choice to do so! Some people draw the purpose of life from their work—cool. Whether that is working for someone else or working for themselves. What works for you is what works for you; you have the freedom to have that choice. And this is where the info in this book is most potent...it allows you to earn and maintain that control over your life.

We come into the military by choice, which enters us into a dictatorship of others telling us how high and when to jump. When we raised our right hand and signed our name on the dotted line, that is the truth and the future. We gave up most of our control, which can be unnerving. And with that, people assume that they have given up control of their financial life and that Uncle Sam will provide and care for them financially. Oh boy, get ready for a rude awakening! NO! Ya jackwagon, you have 100% control over your financial life while in the military—you just need to educate yourself on proper management in order to get the most out of your military journey. But, you have freedoms...you can choose to give up control. If that is the case, close this book and return it because it is not for you. This book is about returning that control to you!

So, we have multiple options on this journey regarding retirement. We must identify what we want to achieve and take the reins. Here are some of the options:

○ Stay in 20+, work another job post-military, and retire at 60.

○ Stay in 20+, work to be financially savvy, and completely retire at 20+.

○ Separate early and retire early.

They are all possible, and some possibilities aren't on that list. You just need to take control of your financial life, have that intestinal fortitude to work towards your financial goals, and make it happen for you. There is no handholding here. You must put in the hard work, set your goals, and make it all work for you. This book will be your guide in making that journey.

Putting it All Together

So, in summary. Your life is 100% different from your parents and your grandparents. I don't want to say that they had it easier because they had different challenges in life than you do today. But, they at least had more of a set and defined financial path to follow than we and our future generations will ever have. We need to stop carrying forward that archaic formula that will never work again!

From this point on, we start anew. We stop taking financial advice from Uncle Dale who is not wealthy himself, and in turn, we must seek to grow our financial literacy from those who have accomplished what we strive to achieve.

We stop thinking that college is the end-all be-all for a wealthy future; we must blaze our tailored paths forward towards what works for us and how we would like to see our financial retirement. Money doesn't buy us happiness but it fuels those passions that give us joy and fulfillment…so…I guess it does buy happiness…by the way, that saying is meant to keep us poor by programming us to think that we should not strive money…but that topic is for another book.

Final Mindset Notes to Ponder

Above, we worked on a significant mindset flaw that most of us have learned since we were young. Below are some other mindset traits to ponder and uncover throughout this book. And the following mindset traits are ones that wealthy people have while poor people do not. Thank you, Robert Kiyosaki, for compiling these:

○ *The poor work for money, while the rich have money to work for them.*

○ *The rich build assets, while the poor focus on acquiring liabilities (debt).*

○ *It is not about how much money you make; it is about how much money you keep for yourself.*

○ *The rich minimize the impact of taxes while the poor pay large percentages of taxes.*

○ *The rich seek or create opportunities and take risks, while the poor value security and safety.*

○ *The rich let their habits and goals guide their emotions, while the poor let their emotions guide their goals and habits.*

○ *The purpose of money is to bring us security and peace of mind. When you are stuck with a financial decision, ask yourself, "What will make me feel most secure?" Is it saving more in an emergency fund or investing riskier to get me to where I want to be quicker?*

How do those points make you feel? When I first discovered those traits, I thought, "Wow, I need to get my ass in gear!"

I hope to walk you through the benefits of these traits within these pages. Keep them in mind, let them be guideposts, and revisit them as they are crucial on our journey.

Enough about mindset. For now, let us press forward and set our journey ahead in a new and more productive light!

Homework

What are your limiting beliefs that are holding you back?

_____

_____

_____

_____

Who do you need to stop listening to because they are not where you want to be in life?

_____

_____

_____

_____

What are your biggest takeaways from this chapter?

_____

_____

_____

_____

_____

_____

Action Items

1. Identify your limiting beliefs around finances and begin to change them.

What are your biggest takeaways from this chapter?

_____

_____

_____

_____

_____

Action Items

Take a moment to think... and begin to change them.

CHAPTER 2

Oh Hot Damn, Budgeting

As military members, we all start out sucking at budgeting. Yes, I am looking at you, that guy in love with Cinnamon down at the local strip club, to the miss with a 36% interest loan on a new Dodge Charger, to Sgt. Blackout who spends way too much on liquor every week. If we want to be financially healthier, we all need to bite the bullet and learn to budget.

NOW! Let me make this clear. Budgeting alone will not make you a millionaire. I will not tell you that you need to cut out your Starbucks completely or only eat instant noodles. Some choose to do that, and that's fine. But it doesn't work for everyone. It is a process; a way of life to learn how to budget. So, from this point on, we all need to agree not to be hard on ourselves when we slip up. We just need to strive to get better every day and focus on the things that bring us value and keep us whole. (This will make more sense in a little bit.) We need to set ourselves up on a solid path that leads towards our financial goals and not further away—that is what budgeting accomplishes.

What is Budgeting?

At the heart of it all, budgeting is a devised plan for spending your money. Let us go one step further because that is too boring and surface-level. We want all our money working towards our goals, and that is what a "Zero-Based Budget" accomplishes.

A Zero-Based Budget is where we end up with $0 when we subtract our spending from our income. This lets us know that every one of our dollars is working towards our goal. In this chapter, we will work through building a solid Zero-Based Budget!

Mindset Check – It is best to think of yourself as a business. "You, Incorporated!" Every corporation or business needs to keep track of various ratios, financial statements, and reports to properly monitor the company's health and finances. In addition, it should provide insight on where to allocate capital (money) to run efficiently. That is what you are doing with a budget—developing a system to monitor the "health" of your business, i.e., yourself!

Zero-Based Budget

$$\$0 = Income - Expenses$$

Income. That is the simple equation we must begin with to start building our budget. Our income in the military is anything to include basic pay, Basic Allowance for Housing

(BAH), submarine pay, jump pay, etc., and it is super simple to find your income. It is the monthly total on the left side of your LES. This is the easiest part of your budget.

Expenses. This is not so straightforward, even though it is as simple as what you spend your income on. There are so many expenses that we must account for and keep track of, but we can make that process a little simpler. Let's expand that formula a little further to help us:

$$\$0 = Income - [\text{Living (Fixed)} \; Expenses \\ + Adjustable \; Expenses + Debt + Taxes$$

This may look even more confusing, but it is super simple, so hold your horses. Living, or "Fixed" Expenses as they are sometimes called, are expenses that have a constant cost every month and are hard to adjust in a short amount of time! Think expenses with a contract surrounding them (insurance, rent, mortgage, etc.). Adjustable expenses are everything else—expenses that change from month to month; allow you to have fun. You can adjust them quickly; you can use the money to blow your paycheck at the local strip club… but seriously…don't do that, but you can. If it makes you happy, budget it! Examples:

Fixed/ Living	Adjustable
Rent/Mortgage	Groceries
Utilities	Restaurants
Insurance	Travel

*"If you buy things you do not need, soon you will
have to sell things you need."*

– *Warren Buffett*

Taxes. Oh boy, everyone loves taxes.

*"In this world, nothing can be said to be certain,
except death and taxes."*

– *Benjamin Franklin*

Taxes are here to stay. As much as we would love them just
to pound sand, they will always be here. So, we need to make
sure that we budget them in. And sadly, they are an expense
that we must account for. Fortunately, as military members,
we have some perks regarding tax expenses in our finances,
mainly dealing with state taxes and untaxable income—*woo-
hoo!* But we will dive into this shortly.

If you are lucky enough to be stationed in a state that waives
state income tax for military members, I recommend keeping
your residency there. These can change from time to time, so
I will not list them here; check with your branch's personnel/
finance section to help guide you.

Taxes can take 30% to 40+% of our hard-earned income.
And from our mindset chapter, paying as little as possible
in taxes is one facet of the game. Please consult with a tax
representative familiar with military taxes to help lower your
taxable income.

Debt. We have all had it in our lives, and it must be accounted
for. Debt is a very polarizing topic. Many online personalities

say that ALL debt is evil, and we should work to pay it off quickly. Then another group of folks believes that smart debt is good to have, while removing dumb debt. What do I mean by smart and dumb debt?

Smart Debt – Debt with an interest yield (APR/APY) of less than 5% that grows you personally or financially, or if your APR is less than the return of an investment in the stock market (~8%). This is mainly mortgages (we will talk about them soon).

Dumb Debt – Debt with an interest yield (APR/APY) of greater than 5% that harms you personally or financially, or if the APR is more than the return of an investment in the stock market (~8%). This is mostly consumer debt (credit cards, payday advances, etc.).

So, a few examples:

1. You have a mortgage of $120K, with an APY of 3.2%, with a $500/month payment.

   Smart Debt – I would not rush to pay off my mortgage when I can return 8% (100-year average of market returns) annually. So, by using OPM (Other People's Money), you can invest that $120K+ additional income outside of $500/month, earning 4.8% [8% to 3.2%] annually.

2. You have two credit cards with a combined balance of $12K, with an APY of 25.4%.

   Dumb Debt – I would pay this off as quickly as possible. (We will go into this strategy later.) You *can* make more than 25.4% in the market, but it is unlikely for most and will eat into your earnings from investing. Pay this debt off quickly!

3. Taking out a $20K loan to pay for an investment/self-improvement course at 5.5% APR.

Smart Debt – Your APR is a little high but not detrimental. If you select a reputable course, then the return on investment (ROI) of learning a new skill will pay a higher ROI in the long run than the loan price. Would you take that investment if you can pay $20K today on a skill that will make you $100K in one to two years?

People fall into a mindset trap of "I can't invest until I pay off all my debt." If you fall into this trap, you will lose out on so much growth. Sort your debt, capitalize on the smart debt, and lower your dumb debt to become financially healthier.

The one piece of debt that is the most dangerous to you is student loan debt. And honestly, it is seriously fucked up that this is a rule baked into student loan debt. But the reason why it is so dangerous is that 95% of the time it will not go away if you declare bankruptcy or die. You can never reset from it, unlike most other debts. You cannot start anew through bankruptcy and it can be passed onto your heirs... super shitty. So, focus on paying off that credit card debt first (high interest) and then knock out that student loan debt. Almost everything else can wait.

Military Perk with Debt – If you enter the military with active loans, look up the Servicemember's Civil Relief Act. If that active loan's interest rate is higher than 6%, creditors must limit the interest rate to 6%! Call them and get that changed; that can help you out big time!

We will talk about it here, and that is debt repayment. There are two main strategies when tackling debt, and they both have to do with snow – snowball and avalanche. These strategies are used when you have more than one form of debt…if you just have one…it makes it a lot easier…science.

The debt snowball strategy focuses on the total debt size as a priority, while the debt avalanche strategy focuses on the highest interest incurring loan as a priority. Here is a little more detail on how to apply each:

Debt Snowball	Debt Avalanche
1. Make the minimum payment on each debt, monthly	1. Make the minimum payments on each debt, monthly
2. Make extra **principle only** payments on the smallest balance loan	2. Make extra **principle only** payments on the highest interest debt
3. When the first loan is paid off, move to the next highest balance loan/debt	3. When the first loan is paid off, move to the next debt with highest interest rate

*Note: I highlighted "principle-only" for a reason, any EXTRA payment on ANY debt, should be set to principle-only, this is something you can do when you call the institution/bank when submitting your payment. Selecting principle-only ensures that you are paying down your loan quicker and not just the debt incurred.

For both strategies, after you pay off the first debt, you take that minimum payment from the first debt PLUS any extra payment you made and add that to the minimum payment of your second debt. There for, you increase the speed of which you are paying off your debt. If you have more debt, continue to add the payments on top of each other and you will be done in no time.

Now, which one is better? I would choose the debt avalanche strategy any day; over the life of the loan, you are spending less money as you are saving your loans from climbing due to the addition of interest. BUT! If you need the motivation, the snowball strategy is great because it allows you to have those short-term wins by paying off smaller loans first, which may keep you in the game. But, if you have the strength to stick with it for the long-term, go with the debt avalanche as your strategy.

Check out my website, where I have an outstanding debt-tackling spreadsheet that can help you chart your strategy to get out from under debt!

Building Your Budget Tracker

Step 1: Use Google Sheets (free for everyone) or Microsoft Excel. (You can get a free copy through the military for your personal computer.)

Step 2: Find a budget template online or in Microsoft Excel and mirror your favorite template.

Step 3: Print off your bank accounts for the past three to six months, including credit cards. Classify each purchase as a category (i.e., groceries, recreation, rent, etc.). Add all the charges within those categories, and then divide the total by the number of months used (i.e., three-month data, divide the total by three) to get your average per month cost.

Step 4: Massage your average category costs to make them work for your situation.

Step 5: Allocate your money to a category. Pay yourself 10% of your income FIRST! Then allocate any leftovers to savings or investments to get $0.

Step 6: Pat yourself on the back—all your money is working for you. Check in monthly or every couple of months to see if you are on track and adjust if needed.

> *"Do not save what is left after spending, but spend what is left after saving."*
>
> *– Warren Buffett*

Financial Health Indicators

Ok, cool, so we have a budget. It works for us; but is what works for us genuinely healthy for our overall budget? Let's explore that.

Corporations and businesses spend quite a bit of money monthly, quarterly, and annually to make sure that they are in a healthy financial position to move into the future. They do this through countless metrics and ratios compared to a benchmark standard. If they are outside of those standards, then they take the time to course-correct. If we treat ourselves and our financial situation as a business or a corporation, then we should take the time to do the same.

It's very important to keep tabs on how you are doing in this crazy financial life!

Warning! The upcoming pages will have mathematical equations...they are not as scary as they appear...toughen up, buttercup, and we will push through together!

1. Emergency Fund

   There are multiple levels to an emergency fund. $1K, three months, six months, and 12 months (optional).

   Surprise! This isn't even a formula. Everyone should have at least $1,000 stashed away as an emergency fund.

   Why? Part psychology and part preventing derailment of goals. If you have $1,000 stashed away in a savings account, you don't have to dip into your investments to pay for emergencies that take away potential returns. But, also, it is a piece of mind that you have funds to protect you at a low point.

Now…let's get this straight. Emergencies are not "I need this new PlayStation, I overspent on my restaurant budget, so I need to pull from here."

An emergency is, "I just blew out two tires on my ride into work, I need to buy plane tickets to see my dying grandmother, etc." It is not an emergency if you do not get that new gaming console. Glad we got that straight!

Once you have your $1K saved, work to save three months' worth of mandatory expenses (rent, debt payments, food, utilities, etc.), anything to sustain life—no "fun" things. This is in case life happens, such as you get kicked out of the military and have trouble finding a job right away.

If it brings you more comfort in life to know that you have more than three months of funds saved, then do that, but it's not mandatory for everyone. Unless you are planning on separating soon, I would recommend saving at least six-month's worth in a High-Yield Savings Account (HYSA) because the civilian job market is not as secure as the military, especially during a recession or just getting a job with a shitty company.

Note: What I would do is hold the $1,000 in a savings account with your bank to have easy access to it in an emergency. For the rest, focus on getting your investment accounts up to $10,000 so you have money working in the market. Then, start saving a larger emergency fund if it brings you comfort.

2. Current Liquidity Ratio

$$Current\ Liquidity = \frac{Cash}{Debt}$$

Goal = Minimum 1–2, Higher is Better

This formula is one that corporations use all the time. It shows how much cash we have on hand relative to debt amount. Cash includes non-retirement investments, savings, checking accounts, etc. Any type of cash that we can get to quickly (within 24–48 hours). Debt is all debt—smart or dumb.

This ratio aims to calculate how many times you can pay off your current debt load with your current cash reserves.

If you are below one, then make the effort to burn off your debt. Focus on that checklist step until you get above one on your current liquidity ratio.

3. Basic Housing Ratio

$$Basic\ Housing = \frac{Housing\ Costs}{Gross\ Income}$$

Goal = Less than 28%

> *Note: Gross means before taxes or any other deductions are removed, so the bottom total of your income block is on the left-hand side of your LES (Basic Pay, BAH, BAS, etc.) Your net income is taxes and deductions removed. So, your right-hand side totals on your LES.*

This is an excellent check to ensure that we are not living above our means. This goes for both rental and owning a house. For owning a home, make sure that you include your principle, insurance, tax, and interest within your housing cost. Housing cost for rentals is really just your rent payment and rental insurance.

If you are over 28%, you need to investigate moving (once your lease is up) to a cheaper place because you live way above your means, or get a roommate to help split the cost! When I discovered this ratio…I lived at 30% and moved once my lease was up, and I began living a lot more comfortably!

4. Total Debt Ratio

$$Total\ Debt = \frac{Total\ Liabilities}{Total\ Assets}$$

Note: Assets = cash + checking + savings + investments + owned assets at fair market value (furniture, house, car, etc.)

You are aiming for less than one. Anything more than one and you live WAY above your means and need to lower your debt ASAP!

But this ratio measures the performance of your budgeting. If your budgeting is indeed working, you should see a decrease in this ratio from year to year until you eventually reach zero!

5. Savings Rate

$$Rate = \frac{Savings + Investment + Employer\ Match}{Gross\ Monthly\ Income} \times 100$$

Note: Employee match is the percentage of your income that the government matched for your TSP. Investments are what you contribute to your investment accounts. Again, gross is before taxes are taken out.

The savings rate is a percentage of your monthly income that you are saving monthly for the future. You could have guessed that from the title. Huh!

The benchmark for the percentage varies by your age; these are the minimums you should be aiming for— you can go higher if you'd like. Please just enjoy life a little and do not purposely eat instant noodles for every meal...also not a shit hot way to pass your PT test.

Age	Saving Rate Minimum Goal
25–35	10–13%
36–45	13–20%
46–70	20–40%

6. Investing to Pay Ratio

$$Investing\ to\ Pay\ = \frac{Investment\ Assets + Cash}{Annual\ Gross\ Pay}$$

This may seem like the savings rate, but this ratio is a way to see if you are saving enough in your investment accounts to meet your needs upon retirement. Your investment assets and cash are the totals that you currently have! It is easiest to do this towards the end of a year, as you will use your gross annual pay and your year-end total of cash and investment accounts to calculate.

Age	Investing-to-Pay Minimum Ratio Goal
25–30	0.2
31–35	0.6–0.8
36–45	1.6–1.8
46–55	3–4
56–65	8–10
65+	16–20

If you are getting lower than the minimum goal in your age bracket, then you can do multiple things:

1. Lower debt to allocate more to savings.
2. Find other means to increase investment savings (adjust the budget, increase income to increase savings rate).

Example:
You are 32. Your gross pay is $85,000 per year. You have $1,000 in cash (in your checking and savings accounts). And $50,000 in your retirement accounts, a total of $51,000.

$$Investing\ to\ Pay = \frac{\$\,51,000}{\$\,85,000} = 0.6,\ On\ Target$$

You want to maintain that $85,000 a year income at retirement (age 65, let's say). You contributed 10% of your income every year ($8,500) to your investments with an average market return of 8%. You would have $1,986,305 in your account, which would be an investing-to-pay ratio of:

$$Investing\ to\ Pay = \frac{\$\ 1,986,305}{\$\ 85,000} = 23.4,\ On\ Target$$

Well done, you are sitting pretty. But I know many of you will do better than this in life!

Cash-Based Budget

I wanted to make sure I hit on what I call a "cash-based budget." It has helped me multiple times in my financial journey, especially when I had a change of income or a change in life (leaving the military was a big one).

A cash-based budget is a pretty simple one. Its purpose is to assist you in sticking to a new budget any time you have an income change or want to shrink your current expenses. Let me just write out the steps. Again, it is so simple, it doesn't take much explanation.

Step 1 – Generate your budget.

Step 2 – Identify your adjustable/variable/etc. expenses, whatever you want to call them.

Step 3 – Add those expenses up, go to an ATM, and pull out that dollar amount in cash.

Step 4 – Tell all those asshats that say, "You still carry cash?" to pound sand. "Who the hell carries cash anymore?" YOU do because you are financially intelligent!

Step 5 – ONLY use that cash for your adjustable expenses! If you run out before the next paycheck... tough luck, do better next paycheck. (Or just subtract your overage from what you pull out next paycheck... eating ramen noodles after you run out just sets the lesson harder!)

Step 6 – Repeat until your finances "stabilize," aka, when you do not go over budget anymore and are used to that monetary lifestyle. You can return to using your credit cards.

Step 7 – If you slip up with your credit card...go back to cash.

That is it. It helped me so much to build my financial habits! I organized a fancy accordion envelope with labels...because I'm a nerd! Ta-da! Welcome to proper budgeting!

Putting It All Together

The mindset is the foundation of your financial house. If the foundation is weak, then the rest of the house will be weak, so we start there. In this chapter, we focused on budgeting, which is like the rough framing of the house. It doesn't make the home beautiful, but it gives it structure and discipline. Without it, it will crumble.

Again, your budgeting skills will not make you a millionaire. They will certainly help, but they are not the end-all be-all. Furthermore, they are not something that is going to be perfect overnight. It took me a solid six months to get my budget stable and to be disciplined. In that six-month window, I was massaging it to find the ground truth and eating a lot of Ramen noodles when I went over budget.

Make it work for you; put in consistent effort to stay on task. Make sure you fall within healthy financial parameters, and begin your journey on your new solid path to reach your financial goals in life!

Homework

What are your largest expenses? Are they essential or are you impressing other people with them?

_____

_____

_____

_____

What is one small change you can make NOW to your budget that would allow you to save and invest more?

_____

_____

_____

_____

What are your biggest takeaways from this chapter?

_____

_____

_____

_____

Action Items

1. Build or download a budget tracking system.
2. Analyze the past three to six months of banking and credit card statements, categorize purchases, and capture those categories on your tracking system.
3. Average each category to find your average spending.
4. Adjust those average spending amounts to meet your life situation.
5. Figure your financial health.
6. Begin tracking your expenses and adjusting monthly.
7. Start a cash-based budget, if necessary.

CHAPTER 3

A Word about Credit

Credit...I wish it didn't, but our financial lives revolve around credit and our credit score. Building your credit should start early in your adulthood, and it should be a calculated thing.

Let's put it this way...say you wanted to take out a 30-year mortgage on a $250,000 house with 0% down (not recommended but easy math). Your low credit score gets you an interest rate of 4.5%, and a high credit score gets you a rate of 4.0%. While a difference of 0.5% doesn't seem a lot, that 4.0% will save you $26,345 over the life of your mortgage. Huge!

Your credit health is expressed using a FICO (Fair Isaac Corporation) score. This is the output of a very fancy formula that shows banks and other loan writing institutions how "creditworthy" you are, or in other words, credit trustworthy, and how willing you are to pay back your loans. Again, a super confusing formula, but here are the main things that affect your score:

1. Amount of Open Accounts
   Low Impact on Score – 11–20+ Open Accounts is
   ideal.

2. Amount of Negative Marks
   High Impact on Score – Bankruptcy, Late/Missed
   Payments, etc. Work with the credit bureaus to fix or
   remove if you can.

3. Average Age of Accounts
   Medium Impact on Score – 9+ Years of Active Credit
   Usage is Ideal.

4. Accounts Paid on Time
   High Impact on Score – Always strive to be on time,
   100%, even a drop to 98% of the time can drop your
   score big time!

5. Amount of Credit Inquiries
   Low Impact on Score – There are two types. Hard and
   Soft…keep your comments to yourself! Hard is when
   you are applying for a brand-new loan or credit card,
   impactful on your score. Soft is when a request for
   your credit history goes through, not impactful. The
   closest to 0 is most ideal.

Credit Usage

High Impact on Score – How much debt you are carrying
on your card as a percentage of your total credit available.
Credit companies give you a "credit balance."—the max that
you can borrow on that credit line. You want to keep that
percentage between 0% to 9%, ideally. Try your hardest
never to go over 30%!

I recommend creating a "Finance" app folder on your phone and downloading the "Credit Karma" app. It is free credit monitoring to identify how your credit score is improving. It shows you the areas you need to work on to improve your score. It will also alert you to any issues (fraudulent accounts, data breaches, etc.). It's a good, all-around financial health tool!

Once your budget is stable (you aren't going over budget for three months straight), then it is time to start using credit wisely. And that means never using your debit cards (except for drawing cash out of an ATM and any expenses that incur a fee if you use a credit card, mainly rent and utilities); you should be using credit cards for your everyday purchases.

This does three things...

1. Credit cards have much better fraud protection—if someone steals your credit card information, the rest of your money reserves are not exposed, and your bank will typically recoup your money quicker on credit than debit.
2. Helps to build your credit score higher.
3. You earn rewards on what you spend, so you get a return on your spending, win-win!

You will hear many online "gurus" speak about the value of "OPM—Other People's Money." And this is what you can do with credit cards. Other people's money is the thought that instead of using your own money that you earn each month, borrow the bank's money (really, other bank users' money) to secure what you need to live. This allows you to utilize your money towards investments during the month, grow your wealth, and pay last month's purchases with next month's funds. This is better utilization of your hard-earned cash.

Now, the catch! You MUST pay your card off each month. If you carry a balance over to the next month and you end up paying high interest, then this strategy is all for nothing—you have wasted money. That is why your budget must be solid before starting this!

In my opinion, everyone should have a credit card or multiple cards. And as military members, we have some perks through the Servicemember Civil Relief Act (SCRA). It means that as military members, if you had loans that were taken out BEFORE starting active duty, then you are entitled to have your interest rate on those loans capped at 6%...which also means you should be reimbursed those interest charges from today and when you started active duty. This goes for all loans (student, car, etc.). Keep this in mind; this can save you hundreds! Call up your bank or loan institution and provide your active-duty information to enact SCRA. The SCRA also has some other perks associated with it, mainly protecting us members from predatory lending or retribution from creditors for joining the military or deploying while on active duty.

So, what is your situation, and what should you do?

Credit Score Less than 580

Focus on building your credit. Find a credit builder card. It won't have many rewards tied to it, but you aren't going for that right now. Once you receive your card, mainly if you haven't used a credit card before, be super careful with your spending. It is easy to overspend if you don't have a solid budget in place or self-control with your swiping.

I would recommend picking a category—i.e., groceries, fuel, etc. Charge your credit card with expenses only in this category and pay it off each month! Easy-peasy!

Tip: If you do get any rewards, match the rewards to the category you will spend the most on (more than likely groceries)!

Credit Score 580 to 670

Begin earning rewards on your spending. Look for a significant cash back card and continue what you were doing while building your credit. But at this point, your rewards should be better for your higher score.

You can either call the bank and ask for an upgrade to your current card or open another. If you stick with the same bank, they shouldn't ding you again on a hard credit pull. And the additional account will only improve your situation if you are disciplined with your spending.

Credit Score above 670

Begin earning perks on top of your rewards! You are looking to gain a premium card at this point. You don't want to try it any sooner because if they decline you, that wasted hard pull on your credit will shaft you and your score.

What are your goals? Do you want to travel more, do you want more cashback on specific activities, etc.? Those are the premium perks you want to focus on in this range.

Other Loans/Credit

Vehicle loans. This is for both used and new. (For the love of God, don't get a new vehicle!) Even if you have the cash, I recommend still getting a loan if you can find a loan under a 3% interest rate (APY) for as long as possible. Use OPM! Work it into your debt strategy (snowball vs. avalanche) that we discussed previously and use that large cash load to invest in an investment that gives you a return more significant than 3%!

Mortgage. Buying a house will be largely dependent on your goals in life. But use your VA loan perks to secure your place. (We will go into more about the VA loan a little later.) This helps as you do not have to remove a large portion of your investment money to make a down payment. According to compoundadvisors.com, over the past 30 years the average home return on investment (ROI) is 2.2% per year. Minus repairs, the return is lower. If you can keep as much of a potential down payment in the stock market (8% average yearly ROI), your money will be working harder for you! But we will explore this more in a chapter coming dedicated to housing.

Personal loan. If you have a large purchase, use these over a credit card! You will still have a higher APY (8% to 12%), but that is excellent vs. your 19% to 30% APY for credit cards. If you need cash for a guaranteed investment (business, etc.), that will give you a return on investment (ROI) more significant than your APY. This is an excellent way to go. Don't fear debt—use it wisely…like a rich person.

Military Perk on Credit – As of January 2022, American Express (Amex), Chase, Citi, and US Bank have all waived their annual credit card fees for active military members. Huge perk, especially if you like to travel. They are great travel cards with unique perks. Do your research to see which is best for you. And if it is still allowed for military travel, charge your TDY/PCS flights to your travel card and enjoy those free miles!

Also, as part of the Military Lending Act (MLA) which protects active-duty service members from predatory lending, all debt cannot have an interest rate higher than 36%—get those adjusted if you do...and for the love of God, avoid debt with a percentage higher than 25%!

Sadly, the above two tips are only for active-duty members on active-duty orders for longer than 30 days—sorry Reserves and Guard, retirees, or separated folks.

Use your card with the highest benefit on a category (groceries, gas, etc.), and occasionally, cash in your points and benefits to get a rebate! Work on your credit correctly and your money will work for you...this is part of the equation to grow your wealth.

Homework

What are your biggest takeaways from this chapter?

_____

_____

_____

_____

_____

_____

Action Items

1. Download Credit Karma or some credit tracking application.
2. Analyze areas that you can fix/improve.
3. Begin and continue building your credit and maintain a healthy level.
4. Monitor your credit every month or every other month.

CHAPTER 4

Housing, Our Largest Expense

While writing this book, I was going to break down housing into each rank's breakdown. But holy shit, there is way too much to go over, and it is the same between all ranks. Housing costs are our most significant expense! That is the same whether we are renting or purchasing a home. And with our most significant expense, we need to take some dedicated room to break it down entirely. So, let's do just that.

To Rent or to Buy?

It is not as simple as: "Do this, not that." It depends on your financial goals, career path, and your current financial situation.

A lot of this decision comes down to time. How much time do you plan on being in this house or apartment? Do you plan on returning to this house at some other point in your career or after you retire/separate? This is important because you tend to lose money on a mortgage for the first three to five years due to the amortization schedule of the loan. Amortization is just fancy speak for:

According to Investopedia, amortization is the process of writing down the value of a loan...the amortization schedule presents a loan repayment schedule based on the loan's maturity date (when it is done/paid off). It highlights the principle (original loan value) of the loan and the incurred interest rate value over the life of the loan. And how the loan is paid down with each payment.

Here is an example of the "average" US mortgage as outlined by Rocket Mortgage and its associated Amortization Schedule:

Home Cost: $272,500
Down Payment (12%) + Fees/Costs: $40,875*
Loan Amount: $239,800
Loan Length: 30 years
Interest Rate: 3.25%
Monthly Payment*: $1,044
*3% of Home Cost for Fees and Costs

Months	Beginning Balance	Scheduled Payment	Principle	Interest	Ending Balance	Cumulative Interest
0	$239,800.00	$0.00	$0.00	$0.00	$239,800.00	$0.00
1	$239,800.00	$1,043.62	$394.17	$649.46	$239,405.83	$649.46
2	$239,405.83	$1,043.62	$396.30	$647.33	$239,009.53	$1,296.78
3	$239,009.53	$1,043.62	$398.44	$645.19	$238,611.10	$1,941.97
4	$238,611.10	$1,043.62	$400.58	$643.04	$238,210.51	$2,585.01
5	$238,210.51	$1,043.62	$402.73	$640.89	$237,807.78	$3,225.91
6	$237,807.78	$1,043.62	$404.88	$638.74	$237,402.90	$3,864.65
7	$237,402.90	$1,043.62	$407.04	$636.58	$236,995.86	$4,501.23
8	$236,995.86	$1,043.62	$409.21	$634.42	$236,586.65	$5,135.65
9	$236,586.65	$1,043.62	$411.38	$632.25	$236,175.27	$5,767.90
10	$236,175.27	$1,043.62	$413.55	$630.08	$235,761.73	$6,397.97
11	$235,761.73	$1,043.62	$415.73	$627.90	$235,346.00	$7,025.87
12	$235,346.00	$1,043.62	$417.91	$625.71	$234,928.09	$7,651.58
13	$234,928.09	$1,043.62	$420.10	$623.52	$234,507.99	$8,275.11
14	$234,507.99	$1,043.62	$422.29	$621.33	$234,085.69	$8,896.44
15	$234,085.69	$1,043.62	$424.49	$619.13	$233,661.20	$9,515.57
16	$233,661.20	$1,043.62	$426.69	$616.93	$233,234.51	$10,132.50
17	$233,234.51	$1,043.62	$428.90	$614.72	$232,805.60	$10,747.22
18	$232,805.60	$1,043.62	$431.12	$612.51	$232,374.49	$11,359.73
19	$232,374.49	$1,043.62	$433.33	$610.29	$231,941.16	$11,970.03
20	$231,941.16	$1,043.62	$435.55	$608.07	$231,505.60	$12,578.10

Above is a snippet of an amortization table. Something that you will see a lot of if you have a mortgage. It breaks down payments and timetables of when your mortgage will be paid off and the total cost of the loan with interest added in! As we can see, the first X year's payments are primarily being applied to interest. You are not making much return.

Let's do another scenario, and we will use the US appreciation average of 2.2% annually with an annual cost for repairs, insurance, and taxes of -2.5% of the home value. Here is what your home value and associated return will look like for you if you decide to sell your home with a 6% selling fee (standard around the US) plus 1% to 2% in taxes after three years because of a PCS:

After selling, you will walk away from the table with a check for $32,072.76 which is not bad. But you wouldn't be able to make another 20% down payment on another home with that amount. However, if you took that initial down payment of $40,875, added the annual repairs, taxes, and insurance that you saved if you rented and invested into an investment fund, and you invested like we are going to show you in later chapters, earning 9.5% annually (11.5% to 12%, accounting for rental insurance and taxes), then you would have an investment fund with a total of $88,246 at the end of three years.

Now! If your life goal has always been to own a house, you are in a career that does not PCS you often, or you want to stay in this location after the military, AND you can afford the costs, then it is okay to purchase. But we need to do it smartly!

1. Do not allow your mortgage, insurance, taxes, repairs, etc. to exceed 28% of your total monthly or annual income.

2. Hunt around for the best interest rate! If you do all your mortgage shopping within 14 days, then you will only have one inquiry on your credit report, no matter how many mortgages you apply for within those 14 days!

3. If you pay any additional money on top of your minimum monthly payment, make sure you make that extra money a "Principal Payment." AKA pays down your loan, not your interest.

4. Always do a 30-year mortgage! Yes, you are going to pay more in interest over the long run:

Length:	30-Yr	15-Yr
Balance:	$250,000	$250,000
Down Pmnt:	5%	5%
Interest Rate:	3.5%	3.375%
Monthly Pmnt:	$1350	$1967

$617 saved per month on 30 years vs. 15 years.

Invest that $617 per month in the market at 8%.

After 30 years invested = $874,667.37.

Interest Gained on Loans:	30 Yrs.	15 Yrs.
	$146.5K	$65.5K

So, by taking the 30-year mortgage, you pay $81K more in interest. But you could grow your monthly payment difference into nearly $875K over the 30 years!

Which would you rather do?

5. If you still know that you will move every two to three years, it means you are more than likely that you are going to be turning your primary residence into a rental property at some point. Keep the 2% rule in mind. (This is overly simplistic—there is much more that goes into pricing a rental property, but that could be another book!) The 2% rule is:

$$2\% = \frac{Gross\ Monthly\ Rental\ Income}{Purchase\ Price\ of\ Property} \times 100$$

You can estimate the rental income by searching for similar houses being rented in your area online. Note: 2% is the best; some areas are hard-pressed to reach much above 1%. What you use (2% vs. 1%) is based on your needs and wants, and either will do you well over shopping blindly.

What I did for two of my assignments was the "house hacking" version of buying. I purchased a duplex and a triplex multi-family house. I lived in one of the apartments and rented out the rest. There are some advantages, from tax savings to additional income. But there are some headaches with needing to have a much larger reserve for repairs and just dealing with people and their lives. A property manager can help with this if you don't want to deal with it, but this option is not for everyone! Check out biggerpockets.com; they have some great books and other resources to help you if this sounds appealing to your investing future! Biggerpockets is where I gained much of my education in real estate investing, combined with the school of hard knocks. But I won't get into it in this book because that could be a whole additional book on top of this one! I know a few people who did this at every assignment and turned them into pure rentals when they PCS'd, and they had a great income post-military!

Quick Rule of Thumb:
If you are going to be in a location for less than five years -> Rent
If you are going to be in a place for longer than five years -> Buy
In between, it's up to you, but always rent if you are unsure!

Housing – Shifting from Liability to Asset

This is a pro-level move. I did this for five years in my career, and I could have done it better, so I wanted to make sure that I tell you about it. This pro-level move is called "house hacking."

House hacking, as defined by Biggerpockets.com, is "the real estate investing strategy whereby you purchase a property for a low percentage down, live in one part of the property, and rent out the other parts, such that the rent from your tenant (or roommates) exceeds your expenses."

The benefit of this is that it could help cut your housing costs or even eliminate them if the financials are correct. You can either do this with a duplex, triplex, fourplex, or just a single-family house where you have roommates. And the benefit of doing this is that you can buy any one of these properties with a VA loan—a win-win for a military member who wants to pursue this. Especially if you want to get into real estate investing one day—this is a good place to start getting your feet wet. But, it is not for everyone. Like I said, I did it for five years…and chose not to do it again. It was stressful for me, and I went in without adequately investigating the financials and did not turn a profit in the end. I have learned a lot since then—if I could go back those five years, it would be a completely different ballgame.

Pros of House Hacking	Cons of House Hacking
1.) Lower/eliminate personal housing expense	1.) Running a business will take up more of your time or money
2.) Tax benefits for repairs and upkeep of your house	2.) Larger emergency fund needed for repairs
3.) Building equity on your money	3.) More work to select a cash flow positive property
4.) Entry into real estate investing (if that is your thing)	4.) Live with others—if that doesn't bother you then never mind

I am not going into much more detail here—house hacking could be its own book, plus, there are already some great ones out there. Do your research like any investment. A great website is Biggerpockets.com. Get on the forums, find someone who has done it before and see if they will be your mentor. They also have some great tools and books to further your education!

Note: If you use a VA loan to purchase your house hacking property, it must be your primary residence for at least one year, so expect to live in it for more than a year before you are able to rent out the portion that you currently live in!

VA Home Loan

It would be against the law if we had a chapter based on "housing" and did not talk about the VA loan, which I have already mentioned a few times!

The VA home loan is a home loan that the US Department of Veterans Affairs (VA) guarantees, which gives veterans, service members, and some military spouses a loan that has a $0 down payment requirement. This is great, as most home loans require a down payment from 3.5% to 20% of the total home value!

VA Home Loan	Traditional Home Loan
0% down payment	Up to 20% down payment
No PMI required	PMI required*
Competitive interest rates for everyone	Best interest rates for those with high credit score
Easy to qualify	Stricter qualification standards
Lower closing costs	Standard 2% to 3% closing costs

* PMI – Private Mortgage Insurance. On a traditional loan, when you cannot pay the full 20% down, you must pay PMI to the bank for the increased risk they take on by approving you…and you do not get it back.

There is a "funding fee" that is attached to the loan, which goes straight to the VA to continue to fund the ability to have a VA loan in the future. The VA funding fee is 2.3% of the purchase price for your first home on the VA loan. If you add a second home, the funding fee goes up to 3.6% for any other houses bought after the first. With one major caveat: if you have a disability rating from the VA due to a service-connected injury, this funding fee is waived!

You can technically have more than one VA loan (no more than three) out at once, which is another major perk. But it all depends on how much of your VA loan benefits you have used up/are available to you after your first home. It can be a complicated math problem, but in essence, the average veteran receives a total VA loan limit of $647,200 as of 2022. (This goes up based on your county and cost of living there. The maximum is $970,800.) So, if the price of your two homes is less than or equal to your county's limit, then you can take a VA loan on both. Woo Hoo!

It is a precious tool if you dream of owning a home or investment property that you want to live in! Also, once you separate or retire, some states waive property tax if you are 100% disabled—another massive win!

And there you have it. There is my little note on housing in the military. I hope this chapter helped you break down and fully understand your options involving our largest expense that we will encounter in our budget.

Homework

What are your biggest takeaways from this chapter?

_____

_____

_____

_____

_____

Do you need to take any steps to improve your housing situation? If so, what?

_____

_____

_____

_____

Is your current rent/mortgage payment beneficial for your budget?

_____

_____

_____

_____

Is it better for you to buy or rent at this moment in time?

_____

_____

_____

_____

CHAPTER 5

The Basics

The basics…this will pertain to everyone at any point in their military careers. If we are being honest, I put this in here because I didn't want to copy and paste it into every rank's checklist. This will save both of our precious time.

Step A: Set up Your Budget; Build the Budgeting Habit

Pay Yourself First

First Step – Put 10% of your check into your savings or investments.

Here is the order of what savings you should focus on. Once done with the first step, move to the next, and so on:

- ○ $1,000 emergency fund.
- ○ 5% of your pay to your Roth TSP every month.
- ○ Pay off debt (greater than 5% interest rate) using your choice of debt repayment strategies (see Budget – Debt section).

○ Save three to six months of mandatory expenses (rent, utilities, food, etc., not fun money) for Loss of Income Fund; combine this with paying off debt. The military may seem stable to not have to do this, but you never know with the stability of the government in the future or just life events derailing your plans! This helps you pay bills while you find another job without having to dip into your investments...with a caveat! Three months is the minimum, but do what brings you comfort.

What I did – If you have more than $100K in a brokerage account (a non-retirement account), then save your Loss of Income Fund in a high-interest savings account. (Personally, I would only do this with three months' worth.) If you have less than $100K, save your Loss of Income Fund in a brokerage account. You want your money to be working hard below $100K. Is this riskier? Yes. If it bothers you, save it in a savings account. It is all based on your comfort level.

○ Open a Roth IRA, work up to max annual contribution (2022–$6,000 for single/year).

○ If you haven't already, open a Traditional Brokerage Account for your Loss of Income Fund and/or further investing.

These steps will take years to finish—they will not occur overnight. Have patience and stay consistent. Always take steps to grow yourself, even if you slip up on your budget, it happens...believe me.

I will maintain a list of reputable companies that offer high-yield savings accounts, as well as brokerage accounts. I do not want to list them here because it is an ever-changing environment.

Fill in Living/Fixed Expenses

Your living/fixed expenses will be one of the most extensive impacting budget sections throughout your life. Early on in your career, not so much, but the mindset and habits you build around this area will be impactful well into the future!

Housing – Stay in the dorms for as long as possible, if that applies. If you are out of the dorms, find a place with roommates and split rent. (It doesn't work overseas, so enjoy your OHA.) And be smart with your housing costs if you buy or rent with your spouse, partner, and/or kids.

Vehicle – Cheap, cheap, cheap! If you live on base, just get a bike or scooter! But if you must have a car, this is not the time to get a 26% interest Camaro…this will derail your financial future faster than anything else!

Utilities – If you are in the dorms, you don't have to worry about utilities besides maybe your internet and cell phone. Don't go overboard here; get what you need to live your life. It's as simple as that!

Insurance – Do you have debt or a family (wife and kids only)? If so, life insurance is a must. Take the SGLI amount to allow your debt to be paid off if you die, or the SGLI amount to help support your remaining family for a year+. If you don't fit any of those, you don't need the SGLI…it is not an investment because you MUST die to use it.

General Rule of Thumb 1: Focus on meeting your needs, not exceeding them.

General Rule of Thumb 2: Insurance is insurance, investments are investments, just don't mix the two. Aka, "investment-grade life insurance." Just don't!

Fill in Adjustable Expenses

I will not tell you to eat Ramen noodles and not get your fancy coffee. You are young, have fun! If that fancy coffee brings you joy in the morning, makes you more personable, and allows you to network and build stronger relationships, then get that coffee—just budget it in!

Do the things that bring you joy but be mindful of *FOMO*. Always focus on your financial goals. If you want to drop $3K on a travel package, plan for it, save up for it and budget it. Don't just drop that charge at a moment's notice.

Strip that Ego! Shop cheap—groceries are the same at Walmart as they are at Whole Foods; you will just save money on your bill. Now, be mindful of buying other goods at discount stores. It is better to pay more for quality once than it is to pay for budget goods multiple times!

Allocate Rest to Savings/Retirement

After subtracting your expenses from your income, whatever you have leftover, allocate back to your savings and investment goals. The more you have leftover, and therefore the more you save and invest, the quicker you will reach your goals.

Step B: Find Your Financial Risk

Just like doing any activity in life, risk is involved. This goes with your finances especially. Risk in terms of finances is based on how much you can risk losing in your investment during a market crash or downturn.

Risk comes in two parts: a) the type of asset and b) the size of the asset…and it all comes down to confidence! We will dig into this in greater detail later. But a quick, simple thing to remember as we go through the rest of the book is:

1. DO NOT invest in something that you are not confident in—this is where research comes in. If you want to take on more risk, and therefore, a high potential return, choose riskier investments…but, make sure that you still fully understand the investment(s) you are going with.

2. DO NOT bet your whole portfolio on one asset, even if you are super confident! I would say 20% MAX in one position at a time. The more confidence or the more risk you are willing to take, take the more prominent position.

But, like I always say, pick the risk that will allow you to sleep best at night.

Step C: Determine Your Financial Goals

Goals are what allow us to live productive and fulfilling lives. We tend to lose purpose when we are not actively working to achieve a personal goal in life. You see this almost every day with retirees. Their lives and health tend to go downhill and give up the ghost faster once they retire. Most of them also retire their goals at the same time, their bodies and mind are not progressing positively to daily achieve, so therefore they begin to faulter. Always have a well-established goal, and make daily choices to strive to achieve them, you will be a MUCH healthier and happier person!

This is huge in your finances—it helps to keep emotions out of investing. These emotions are the one thing that will cripple us in our investing life. I.e., "Oh, fuck, the market is falling, ABANDON SHIP!" Or, "Wow, Reddit is saying Huggies LLC is going to be the shit and going to the MOON! Invest all my money because of FOMO!" Yeah…come on, all, don't do that!

Set an actionable, achievable, realistic goal, and have a date assigned. Examples:

- Good: "I want to have $500K in my brokerage account by my 35th birthday, making $6,000 per month in returns."
- Bad: "I want to be rich!"

These goals can be anything. They are personal milestones that should reflect and be a bridge to your overall life goals. I want to be able to retire by age 40 and generate a passive income from my investments of $7,000/month so I can move to a new country every few months and live there.

So, my steps…as I am writing this book, I hit 33 this year. My first step is to generate an income of $7K in the next seven years outside of my job. Then I need to sustain it for the rest of my life to live in multiple countries. Actionable, achievable, and realistic!

And with your goals comes your financial risk tolerance! How would you feel emotionally, physically, and mentally if your investments took a 50% dip tomorrow? Usually, the older you get (closer to retirement), the more catastrophic this can be. Losing $10K to a 20-year-old isn't as bad because they have another 40 years to recoup the loss. Losing $10K in the middle of retirement can be the difference between creamed peaches or Friskies cat food…but once you are through with this book, apply it, and reach retirement, $10K will be a drop in the bucket, even for you at 70 years old.

Step D: Develop Strong Credit

Unless your parents were good with credit (mine were not), you would probably be starting from square one. I just need to say one thing, though, because people believe it…CREDIT CARDS ARE NOT FREE MONEY! It is so easy to get carried away with credit cards. You must pay them back, and you need to pay them off in FULL at the end of each month! If you do not, you will be slipping backward each month, not going forward. Make sure you reread Chapter 3 if you are confused about anything.

Start with a primary credit card to help you build credit. Check back with Chapter 3.

Once you have excellent credit (750+), things will come a lot easier for you and, in most cases, cheaper!

Step E: Protect Yourself

We already touched on insurance, so we don't need to beat that dead horse again. This is more along the legal side of it all. And as military members, we have some fantastic opportunities to get this done for free or very cheaply!

There are some mandatory legal documents to protect you and your hard-earned investments, and some are situational. I am not going to pretend to be a lawyer or some estate protection expert, so please follow up the advice with some solid professional legal advice. (This can be free in the military—use it!)

A Word on Deployments

This is something that 98% of the public does not have to deal with, so I wanted to make sure that I cover this because it is unique to us…looking at you, Airman Snuffy. The main perk that we will cover is that when you deploy, you do not have to pay federal taxes, and in some states, there are no state taxes, plus some other perks, woo-hoo! So, here is a quick checklist on deployments from a financial viewpoint:

Pre-Deployment

Done?	Activity
	Keep apartment or move belongings into storage unit? The choice is yours*
	Make sure you update your will, living will, etc. Protect yourself and your money if the ultimate happens. Declare beneficiaries on your retirement and brokerage accounts
	Talk to finance to determine hazardous duty pay, imminent fire pay, and if you keep BAS

Done?	Activity
	Talk to finance about the Savings Deposit Program
	Park your car on base/post and see if a friend can start it every now and then so it doesn't break down (consider putting fuel stabilizer in the fuel tank)

Remember the Military Clause on your rental agreement. If your deployment is longer than 90 days or you gain PCS order (need PCS or deployment orders), you can terminate your lease early. You can place all your goods into a storage unit and pocket your BAH minus storage unit fees. That's right...you get to keep BAH on deployments!

Deployment

Note: Many of these below are only applicable if you are in a "combat zone." Check out current combat zones that qualify for CZTE (Combat Zone Tax Exemption) here https://www.dfas.mil/militarymembers/payentitlements/Pay-Tables/CZ1/ and more about CTZE here https://militarypay.defense.gov/Pay/Tax-Information/CZTE/.

Done?	Activity
	After 30 consecutive days in a combat zone, apply to the Savings Deposit Program (SDP). *—DO NOT go over $10K saved, no benefit past that point

Done?	Activity
	Focus on contributing your annual amount ($6,000/yr. for 2022) to your Roth IRA. In this case, it goes in tax-free while deployed and drawn tax-free when you retire (read more later)—legal double-dipping on tax savings
	This is a great time to save as much as you can! Reformulate your budget when you arrive on deployment to see how much you can realistically commit to the SDP, Roth, and any other accounts

*SDP – This is a DoD-wide program that allows service members to save money **tax-free** while in an active combat zone or a hostile fire/imminent danger pay location. SDP is a savings account pulled from your paycheck to a max of $10K in the account and pays a quarterly interest rate of 10%. I was a dumb ass when I deployed and didn't take advantage of this. I wish I had been a lot smarter back then…hopefully, now you will be much better than I was!

This is a great program. You get a return near what you get within the stock market average. But with the added benefit of having the returns being tax-free! Score! Now, there are many rules…a crazy number of regulations. So, make sure to talk to finance early and visit www.dfas.mil/MilitaryMembers/sdp/ to read up before you head out!

Post-Deployment

Done?	Activity
	Welcome home! Reintegrate into life again, find your housing if you moved out, love your family, and reform your new schedule
	For three months after you return, your SDP still gains interest. After that three-month point, withdraw your funds and apply to your brokerage, or if you need to pay off some dumb debt, do that
	Reformulate your budget to make sure you are still in line with your post-deployment life

Use these perks and advantages to your...advantage. And you could be more set up after you return than when you left for your tour!

Homework

What are your biggest takeaways from this chapter?

_____

_____

_____

_____

_____

What is your:

One-Year Goal:

_____

_____

_____

Five-Year Goal:

_____

_____

_____

Ten-Year Goal:

_____

_____

_____

Action Steps

1. Figure out what step of savings/investing you are on.
2. Analyze if your living expenses are within your means.
3. Identify your financial risk tolerance.
4. Fully develop your financial goals, write them down and live them.
5. Set up a Will (and other recommended legal documents) with your legal office and make sure your insurance is appropriate for your life situation

CHAPTER 6

E1 through E3

Welcome to the military! Most of you are fresh out of high school, ready to take on the world, and since you most likely grew up in the United States, you have absolutely jack squat for financial education...good job US education system!

These are your formative years...these are the years that decide if you will be excellent with money, or shit with money, just based on the habits and mindset you develop during this age and these ranks. So, major kudos for picking up this book...GOLD STAR!

Here is your roadmap to set you up for your military and financial career (even if you don't stay in for 20—no judgment, I didn't).

Two temptations to fight at this point...DO NOT buy a new car, especially at a 35% interest rate...DO NOT get married just to move out of the dorms—no matter how tempting either option is; you will screw over a large chunk of your financial future. Easier said than done, I understand.

DO NOT move on to the next step until you complete the line you are on.

Date of Completion	Activity
	Understand Your LES...sit down with your supervisor and look for mistakes and know what is on there
	If your current state where you are assigned has no state income tax for military members, claim residency there
	Build your budget; keep up with it
	Secure your housing, transportation, and living basics
	Save a $1,000 emergency fund in a savings account. This will take two to four months to complete on average
	5% of paycheck to TSP per month
	Develop your investing style/risk level—implement to TSP
	Begin paying off bad debt (greater than 5% interest). Focus on this completely until your liquidity ratio is above one
	Get your retirement account up to $10K

Date of Completion	Activity
	Build a savings account with three months of bare essential expenses (housing, food, gas, utilities). This will take six months+
	ONCE BUDGET IS STABLE – Open credit-building credit card; spend one budget category (groceries, fuel, etc.) on the credit card and pay off EVERY month
	Open Roth IRA; place remaining funds each month into Roth IRA
	Finalize your will; adjust when you buy a house, get married, have kids, etc.

Homework

What are your biggest takeaways from this chapter?

_____

_____

_____

_____

_____

What is your next step?

_____

_____

_____

CHAPTER 7

E4 through E6

You should have pretty much had your financial habits down-solid from this point on. But now, you are coming into one of your most significant pay raises in your career...be mindful and prevent "lifestyle creep."

Lifestyle Creep — *when an individual's standard of living improves as their discretionary income rises and former luxuries become new necessities, Investopedia.com (2021).*

In other words: more money, new shiny shit to buy.

You will most likely have moved out of the dorms by now and into your first apartment. If you don't have any significant life events (marriage, child, parent moving in, etc.), stay in the same apartment, pocket that BAH bump, and stay with a roommate if you can! If you have a significant life event... yeah, a roommate may disagree with your incoming, more permanent roommate(s).

Date of Completion	Activity
	Continue allocating 5% of income to TSP
	Readjust your budget to match new pay increases! Treat yourself in some places, but focus on increasing your savings and investments
	Bump up your savings account to six months of bare essential expenses, only if it brings you comfort or have a new family/kid(s), or separating soon. Stick with three months if not
	Getting married? Build a wedding savings account or other large purchase savings account...No? Move on, come back when you are
	Having kids? Start saving for college—open an account in their name. Go here to see what type of plan is best for you: https://www.nerdwallet.com/article/investing/529-plan-vs-roth-ira-roth-wins-mostly. No? Move on until you do
	Continue paying off debt and avoid dumb debt
	Maxing out your Roth IRA? Open a brokerage account for extra money

It looks simple because it is! There are so many shiny pennies out there that want to distract us from the simple. And believe me…I have been distracted. And many of you will be too. Here is my advice:

- ○ DO NOT bet the farm on something shiny.
- ○ DO your research so you FULLY understand it. Never put money into something you couldn't explain to a kindergartener.
- ○ DO find someone who can mentor you on the topic and pay them well. Pssst…if you must pay a reputable person to mentor you in something that will positively grow you or your wealth, it is not a bad thing, even if you must take a loan to get that education…keyword REPUTABLE!

I am not even going to touch E7 to E9. Just don't sleep with anyone you are not supposed to, focus on the principles in this book, and you will be golden for the rest of your career!

But in the end, again, money's sole purpose is to provide security and comfort. What will bring you more comfort as you get higher in rank and older in age?

Do you want more savings for peace of mind when you leave the military or if something goes wrong and you must leave unexpectedly? Consider bumping up your savings to 12-months of base essential expenses. Again, this is NOT for everyone, only advisable if it brings more comfort in your life. I knew someone in the service that earned comfort from keeping enough cash in his savings to be able to buy a brand-new car, in case his broke down, he could buy a new one the same day. It is dumb in my opinion and was a shining light on poor financial education that is out there in the military. BUT, it is all his choice, and if that made him feel better, then it is a-ok!

Do you want to be completely retired by the time your 20 years are up? Consider saving more towards your brokerage account, so you can withdraw that money without penalty, unlike your TSP or IRA. Consider starting a business while you are in so it can carry you into retirement as well as more money to fuel your retirement quicker. Consider taking an investing course to help you grow your wealth to freedom-sustaining levels. Head on over to the back of this book and you will find more information on how to explore these options further if they interest you.

One final note that I have for you: Sergeants, you are a supervisor now...having your financial life healthy is more essential for you now than ever before.

> *"You cannot teach and mentor something that you do not do currently; you have no weight behind your words, and no one will follow your example."*
>
> *– Me, I just made that shit up.*

Just for the love of God, do not make your financial health up! As a leader/supervisor, you must teach those below you what you know. And that includes solid financial skills. Yes... it is a real shame that you must guide our younger troops in basic life and adulting skills, but hey, they aren't going to get that from our school system. And not all score big in the parental lottery, so that task falls on you. Learn this, adopt this, apply it, and teach it!

Homework

What are your biggest takeaways from this chapter?

_____

_____

_____

_____

_____

_____

What is your next step?

_____

_____

_____

CHAPTER 8

01 through 02

Welcome to the military, you baby Os! I hope your time at an Academy, ROTC, or OTS/OCS was an eye-opening experience. I would say fun, but we all know if you are looking for "fun," you don't go to an Academy. But, hey, back to finance. Your early officer life is when you solidify your financial health for the rest of your career. Cut your teeth here, and you will be golden.

Let's face it, you are earning a great paycheck coming out of college/OCS. Let's not throw it all away. Your ego will be the #1 downfall of your financial future right here...how do I know? Because I let mine control me...big two-bedroom apartment, a new Jeep Wrangler in my O-1 and O-2 years... aka, pissing money down the drain.

Find comfortable housing that meets your needs, or if you want to accelerate, get a roommate and split all your costs.

Get a humble USED car...NEVER buy a new car until you meet your financial goals. You are pissing money away.

Your checklist will look a little like the E1 through E3 list because you are both new!

There is one big difference! The Career Starter Loan through USAA—game-changer. As of the beginning of 2022, it is a loan for up to $35K for 0.5% interest for Academy grads. For ROTC and OTS, up to $25K for 2.99% interest, perks of Academy. This can be both dumb and smart debt, depending on how you use it. There is also a career-starter loan from Navy Federal, but at the time of writing, it didn't seem as good of a choice. But, please, review both options for updates!

Dumb debt – Using it to buy a new car, purchase furniture, frivolous purchases, etc.

Smart debt – Pay off student debt higher than the interest rate on your Starter Loan, fund your Roth IRA and/or brokerage account, start a business, take a financial course, etc. Are you going to earn more money than what you spend? That is smart.

Note: Don't use for building up savings (emergency, loss of income, etc.) because you do not earn a higher interest percentage on the money in savings than the interest rate on the loan. You want to use it to either lower your current debt load or fund an account or education that will give you a higher rate of return percentage than the loan's interest percentage.

Date of Completion	Activity
	Understand your LES…sit down with your supervisor and look for mistakes and know what is on there
	If your current state where you are assigned has no state income tax for military members, claim residency there
	Build your budget; keep up with it
	Secure your housing, transportation, and living basics
	Save a $1,000 emergency fund in a savings account…will take two to four months to complete on average
	5% of paycheck to TSP per month
	Develop your investing style/risk level—implement to TSP
	Begin paying off bad debt (greater than 5% interest). Focus on this until your liquidity ratio is above 1
	Get your retirement account up to $10K
	Build Savings Account with three months of bare essential expenses (housing, food, gas, utilities) …will take six months+

Date of Completion	Activity
	ONCE BUDGET IS STABLE – Open credit building credit card; spend one budget category (groceries, fuel, etc.) to credit card and pay off EVERY month
	Open Roth IRA; place remaining funds each month into Roth IRA
	Finalize your will; adjust when you buy a house, get married, have kids, etc.

Homework

What are your biggest takeaways from this chapter?

_____

_____

_____

_____

What is your next step?

_____

_____

_____

CHAPTER 9

03 through 04

Your promotion to Captain is the largest financial promotion relative to your other ranks. So, again, work that into your budget, but try and avoid that lifestyle creep! If you can continue to live like a four-year 1Lt for a while longer, you've got it!

This will depend on significant life events (marriage, kids, etc.), but try to live as cheaply and Lieutenant-y as possible!

If you can continue to live with a roommate, do it! Unless you find a wife or have kiddos…you might want to trade that old roommate for your new permanent ones!

But stick with that modest car—no need to get anything flashy. You will never impress anyone with your purchases or impress the "right" people in your life…they really don't give a shit, and they aren't "right" if they do. Adjust your used car purchases with the changing size of your family.

Date of Completion	Activity
	Continue allocating 5% of income to TSP
	Readjust your budget to match new pay increases. Treat yourself in some places, but focus on increasing your savings and investments
	Bump up your savings account to six months of bare essential expenses, optional, but must if having kids, family, or separating soon. Stick with 3-months if not
	Getting married? Build a wedding savings account or other large purchase savings account...No? Move on, come back when you are
	Having kids? Start saving for college, open an account in their name. Go here to see what type of plan is best for you: https://www.nerdwallet.com/article/investing/529-plan-vs-roth-ira-roth-wins-mostly. No? Move on until you do
	Continue paying off debt and avoiding dumb debt
	Maxing out your Roth IRA? Open a bro-kerage account for extra money to balloon investments...and if you are NOT maxing out your Roth IRA by now...you are doing something VERY wrong

I am not even going to continue past O4; you have all the tools in your hand if you develop your habits and discipline in your younger years. Stay the course before your 20th year; you will be very close, if not over the million-dollar mark!

Homework

What are your biggest takeaways from this chapter?

_____

_____

_____

_____

_____

What is your next step?

_____

_____

_____

CHAPTER 10

Thrift Savings Plan (TSP)

Basics

The good ole TSP, or Thrift Savings Plan, was created in 1986 to allow the federal government to mirror the 401(k) plans that corporations were beginning to implement within their organizations. This was great for Civilian Federal Employees but not so much for Military Members back in the day.

Pensions were the name of the game for most corporations before the 1980s. You worked for X number of years, and you received a percentage of your salary for the rest of your life. This was still the name of the game for the US Military until 2018 with the implementation of the "Blended Retirement System (BRS)," when they moved away from the "High-3" Pension system.

The High-3 Pension, so named for the pension, is 50% of your average of the highest three paid years of your salary after 20 years of service (2.5% for each year served). A great incentive for those who want to stay in for 20+ years, but you would receive nothing from your service if you separated early besides the money you saved. Since new military members no longer have the option to enroll within the High-3, we are not even going to cover this.

The BRS was developed to save the government money in the long run by relying on the member to put up funds, provide a match, and lower the amount of retirement % at the end of 20. In addition, it also did the positive of becoming a closer match to a 401(k)-style retirement plan to benefit those with aspirations outside the military. So, just like those who, outside the military, enroll in their company's 401(k), the contributions that they make are compounded by the employer "matching" a pre-determined percentage of their base salary to their 401k fund. For example, if you contribute 2% of your monthly base pay to your 401(k), then your employer will duplicate that 2% to your account. So you gain 4% of your monthly income in your account—a 100% rate of return just from adding to your 401(k)…well, hot damn!

Now, US military members have the opportunity our brothers and sisters have on the civilian side, but with some additional perks: low management fees, ease of use, decent funds if you have a "set it and forget it mentality," and some withdrawal options if you need the cash. Hopefully, you won't until retirement!)

With this being said, this all goes back to what YOUR risk tolerance is and what your financial goals are. Let's break down those next.

The TSP Fund Types

The TSP has six types of funds that you can allocate your money to:

G Fund – Government Securities Fund

Average 10-Year Return*: 1.94%

Mirrors: 10-Year Treasury Rate

Pros: It has little to no fluctuation in price (aka volatility)—very constant!

Cons: The return barely matches inflation, so you technically do not make a return and can lose money if inflation spikes higher than the treasury rate.

Uses: To hold cash in your TSP account—that is it. This is the default account that TSP initially puts your money in. **Make sure you change it when you get in, if the market is positive!**

F Fund – Fixed Income Fund

Average 10-Year Return*: 3.26%

Mirrors: US Aggregate Bond Index (Ticker: AGG)

Pros: Low volatility, not as low as the G Fund.

Cons: Low returns when interest rates are low and poor returns when interest rates spike up.

Uses: This is another fund for holding cash, with a slightly higher rate of return than the G Fund when interest rates are favorable. Use the F Fund when interest rates are flat or falling. The G Fund is better when interest rates rise.

C Fund – Common Stock Index Fund

Average 10-Year Return*: 16.18%

Mirrors: S&P 500 Index (Ticker: SPX)

Pros: Provides the highest consistent rate of return over the long term.

Cons: Fund volatility is dependent on the stock market performance, which can be high at times.

Uses: This will be the primary fund you are invested in within TSP as it provides the most consistent and highest rate of return of all the other funds. This can be your set-it and forget-it fund and dollar cost average, but if you want more hands-on, check out the next section, "Technical Analysis for TSP."

S Fund – Small Capitalization Stock Index Fund

Average 10-Year Return*: 14.98%

Mirrors: Dow Jones US Completion Total Stock Market Index (Ticker: DWCPF)

Pros: Similar rate of returns as the C Fund, with more diversification (can be a con as well) in about 3,300 companies.

Cons: Can have long periods of no returns because of its susceptibility to crashes and bubbles.

Uses: Some will hold a portion of their account in the S Fund to try and return more for their account. We will look at strategies next to see if this is a good tactic.

I Fund – International Stock Index Fund

Average 10-Year Return*: 7.62%

Mirrors: MSCI Europe, Australasia, and Far East (EAFE) Index (Ticker: EFA)

Pros: It allows you some international exposure when the US dollar is weak or US-based companies are falling.

Cons: It is not a representation of the total international market as it only focuses on developed countries (UK, Germany, Japan, etc.) and lacks exposure to emerging markets (small, growing countries).

Uses: When utilizing a strategy that needs international representation, this fund does not fully cover it because most strategies use a whole market (developed and emerging markets) index. Something to keep in mind is that the I Fund will be more conservative as it only tracks about 900 large to medium companies.

L Funds – Lifecycle Funds

Average 10-Year Return: Depends on Your Retirement Year

Mirrors: N/A

Pros: A set-it and forget-it style of investing. Auto adjusts to more conservative holdings (bonds, government securities, etc.) as you get closer to your retirement year with the goal of protecting your wealth.

Cons: No control over your investments. Will return less than the market during uptrends but will lose less than the market during downturns.

Uses: Unless you want the lowest risk possible while returning an *ok* rate of return and don't want to do much work, I recommend the L Funds. If you want more control and a higher rate of return, then don't touch the L Fund and move on to my next section.

Now, the question is, what the hell do you invest in? We will explore the best contribution strategies by analyzing the return of each strategy over 18 years because that is how far the data goes back on TSP gov...funny how that works. Still, it should give us a good feeler for the best allocation strategy since we are investing for the long-term. Let's go!

Fund Allocation Strategies

There are multiple different strategies that you can find online and test out. But guess what, today is your lucky day...I did that for you!

Here are the popular allocation strategies online and their annual CAGR (Compound Annual Growth Rate, best rate to compare different investments strategies) performance over 5, 10, and 18 years. (Twenty years of data is not available.)

S&P 500 Strategy

100% C Fund

5 Year: 18.4%   10 Year: 16.5%   18 Year: 10.7%

Total Market Strategy

80% C Fund & 20% S Fund

5 Year: 20.2%   10 Year: 16.9%   18 Year: 11.0%

The Warren Buffet Strategy

90% C Fund & 10% F Fund

5 Year: 17.7%   10 Year: 15.6%   18 Year: 10.3%

The Dave Ramsey Strategy

60% C Fund, 20% S Fund, & 10% I Fund

5 Year: 16.9%   10 Year: 15.3%   18 Year: 10.4%

The Paul Merriman Strategy

50% C Fund, 25% S Fund, & 25% I Fund

5 Year: 15.9%   10 Year: 14.3%   18 Year: 9.9%

Vanguard Total World Market Strategy

48% C Fund, 12% S Fund, & 40% I Fund

5 Year: 15.3%   10 Year: 13.4%   18 Year: 9.3%

Balanced Index Fund Strategy

48% C Fund, 12% S Fund, & 40% F Fund

5 Year: 14.6%   10 Year: 12.6%   18 Year: 9.1%

Vanguard 3 Strategy

27% C Fund, 7% S Fund, 33% I Fund, & 33% F Fund

5 Year: 12.3%   10 Year: 10.5%   18 Year: 7.9%

50/50 C & S Strategy

50% C Fund & 50% S Fund

5 Year: 16.6%   10 Year: 15.6%   18 Year: 10.9%

As you can see, there are quite a few choices to choose from. And while analyzing the past can give an *ok* glimpse of the future, remember, we don't have a crystal ball, and it is not perfect.

Some strategies work better in the short term and worse in the long term and vice versa. Since, in a TSP we are investing for the long-term, it is better to look at the return of 10+ years.

So, if you would like to have some more control over your account outside of the L Funds, I would use a Total Market Strategy of 80% C Fund and 20% S Fund allocation my whole career.

Initial Investment: $1,000
Yearly Rate of Return: 11.0%
Monthly Contribution: $500
Time: 20 Years

This scenario would leave you with **$415,865.93** at the end of your career. Score! If you are happy with that, then stick with this strategy. But this isn't the actual return on your money because with the Blended Retirement System (BRS), you technically earn more depending on how much you put into your fund monthly! And just for your information, with a difference of .01% (aka 10.9%), you would receive $5,000 less at 20 years than an 11% rate of return.

With BRS came contribution matching. A great thing, especially for those not planning on making the military a career—like this guy!

For your ultimate guide to the BRS, go to militarypay.defense. gov and search "A Guide to the Uniform Service Blended Retirement System."

But we will mainly focus on how much we should contribute to our fund each month. Get all the free money you can get!

	Service Contributions to Your Account		
You put in:	Your Service puts in:		And the total contribution is:
	Automatic (1%) Contribution	Service Matching Contribution	
0%	1%	0%	1%
1%	1%	1%	3%
2%	1%	2%	5%
3%	1%	3%	7%
4%	1%	3.5%	8.5%
5%	1%	4%	10%
More than 5%	1%	4%	Your contribution +5%

Militarypay.defese.gov – A Guide to the Uniform Service Blended Retirement System[3]

We will focus on the second line from the bottom of the above chart; this is where we get the most bang for our buck. For 5% of your Base Pay contributing to your TSP per month, you receive 5% from the government, a total of 10% contribution, and a guaranteed 100% return on your invested money each month.

> *Note: You do not get an automatic 1% contribution until 60 days in the service. The Service Matching Contributions do not kick in until you are 2 years in.*

However, something to keep in mind is that you should be investing in the ROTH TSP primarily! It is the most tax advantageous account for you at a young age. The downside is that any government match will go into a Traditional TSP, which you will have to pay taxes on when you use the money in your retirement. Not the most ideal but not the end of the world. We will get into the difference between Roth and traditional in the next chapter.

Should you do more than 5%? Yes and no. It depends on your goals.

If you want just one account for your retirement and do not wish to do extra work, allocate 5%, then any additional percentage based on your leftovers from your zero-based budget.

If you want to do extra work to turn a more significant percentage on your return, only do 5% because you can do better elsewhere! It's as simple as that!

But, no matter what you do, please read the guide I referred to above. Become educated on what you are investing in. You should NEVER be investing your money blindly because the BRS offers many more perks than what I will be covering here today!

Technical Trading on TSP

This section is not for everyone. It is for those contributing to their TSP who would like to be more hands-on with their investment and increase their returns (no promises, but highly possible). I wish I had created these excellent tools, but the credit goes to my stock investing mentor, Phil Town (2006). Please check out his book or his website to learn more about him.

We defined technical analysis in the Investing Basics chapter of this book, so we aren't going to re-attack that, but technical analysis comes in super handy when dealing with the TSP funds. You can even use this if you took a simple way out and went the L Fund route.

We will be using technical indicators to highlight when we are in for a significant dip in the market, saving us some losses. And by substantial drop, I mean one that comes around every three to five years, not something that happens every day, so you don't have to check it daily.

First, we need to create an account to allow us to view the data we need. Set up an account with Tradingview.com, and sign up for a free account. You won't need a paid account—you've just got to combat a few ad popups. Another great option is TDAmeritrade with their ThinkorSwim platform, a fantastic program. I use it, but it takes a little more time and effort to set up! Check out my website; I may post a setup guide to ThinkorSwim in the future!

Once you are there and your account is set up, here are the steps to see what we need:

1. You will type in "DJI" for the Dow Jones Industrial Average.
2. Next to the ticker symbol, you will select an "M" for the monthly view.
3. Next to "M," select "Candles."

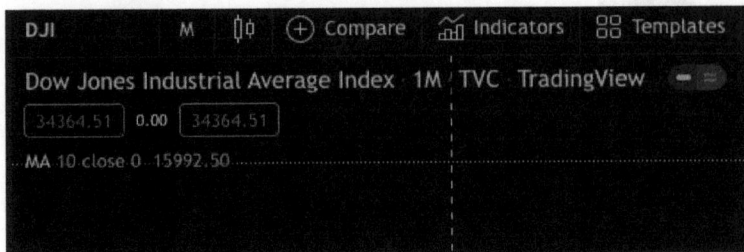

DJI   M   ↕   ⊕ Compare   ⌁ Indicators   ⊞ Templates

Dow Jones Industrial Average Index · 1M / TVC · TradingView   ⊟ ☰

34364.51   0.00   34364.51

MA 10 close 0 15992.50

4. Select "Indicators" at the top of the screen.

5. You are going to search and add the following:

    a. Moving Average (MA).

    b. Moving Average Convergence Divergence (MACD).

    c. Stochastic.

6. Hover over the Moving Average (MA) title on the chart screen and select the cogwheel to change preferences. Do the others the same way.

7. For MA, change "Length" to "10", and keep everything else the same.

8. For MACD – fast length = 8, slow length = 17, MACD length (signal smoothing) = 9, average type = exponential (EMA).

9. For Stochastic – %K Length = 14, %K Smoothing = 5, %D Smoothing = 3, 80% and 20% upper and lower bands under style. Everything else is the same.

What the hell are we looking at?

MA – *Moving Average*

Moving average is an indicator that computes and plots the average stock price over the past X days. So, a 200-Day Moving Average is the average price over the past 200 days planned continuously.

The benefit of this is that it allows you to "smooth" out the price chart by averaging the prices. So, it can enable you to see the actual movement/trend better because it removes the "noise" of spikes and dips in the price that we see on a daily or weekly interval.

We use it because it helps us clearly see a direction change in the market price. Super important!

The "buy signal" is when the candle (price) moves above the 10-day moving average line. Simple. The "sell signal" is when the candle moves below the 10-day moving average line. Done. This is typically the first or second one to flash an arrow.

MACD – *Moving Average Convergence/Divergence*

This one sounds scary and complicated. But really, it takes two Moving Averages and subtracts them to find the difference between the two.

This is the second indicator to highlight a shift in the market, a bullish or bearish shift, just like the MA. But the MACD indicated the strength of the shift through the amount of momentum in the movement. More color = stronger shift; less color = weaker shift.

The "buy signal" is when the bars turn green and/or the blue line crosses above the red. The "sell signal" is when the bars turn red and/or when the blue line crosses under the red line. This is usually the first or second one to flash, depending on the MA.

STOC – *Slow Stochastics*

This is another scary-sounding indicator that is not. It is used to help identify if a stock or index is overbought (above 80%) or oversold (below 20%). Again, a great indicator of a significant bearish or bullish movement in the market.

The "buy signal" is when the red or blue line moves above the 20% line or when the line makes a sharp reversal, making a valley. The "sell signal" is when the lines cross below the 80% line.

Pull all three of these indicators together and you get a power-trio to show you when a substantial drop and a substantial gain (after a decline) are on the horizon, and it is your time to act!

It is as simple as looking for arrows:

- Three red arrows = move your TSP to the G Fund.
- Three green arrows = move back into your Fund(s) of choice.

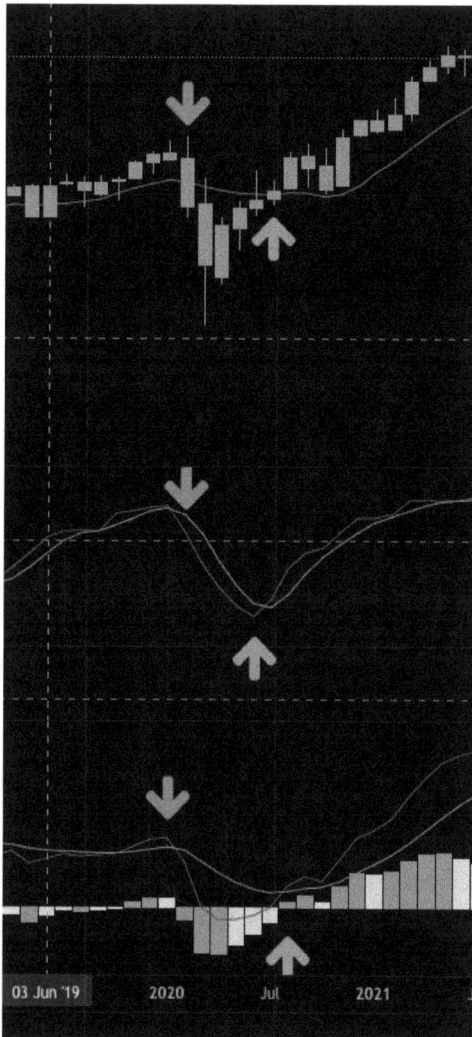

When all three indicators (MA, MACD, and Stochastics) show a red downward arrow and lock in for the current month, (what I mean by "locked in" is since we are viewing this on a time scale of a month, the arrows won't be permanent until the current month ends and the next one begins), that is your indicator to potentially sell your positions (if that is your strategy) and go to cash or G Fund in the TSP—we have a significant downturn or crash looming. Caveat, if there is a significant negative event on the horizon (war, high inflation, looming recession, etc.), you can activate a sell when 2 out of the 3 arrows are present, if you chose to, but it is risky that it could turn around and not collapse. Once the market collapses, then you can do one of two things. You can either guess the bottom and buy back in (very risky but higher return), or take the conservative route and buy back into your indexes and TSP when you have three green arrows return to the indicators.

Put it all together, and this is the rate of return results on the 50/50 Split Strategy, the Total Market Strategy, and the S&P 500 Strategy—since those are the three highest returning:

	50/50 Split	Total Market	S&P 500
18 Yr:	12.78%	12.87%	12.93%

BAM! Squeaking out a few more percentages will get you closer and closer to your goals! And if you go with this technical analysis, go with a 100% C Fund allocation.

Let's take that same scenario that we did before, but with this strategy:

Initial Investment: $1,000
Yearly Rate of Return: 12.93%
Monthly Contribution: $500
Time: 20 Years

You would have a portfolio worth **$526,217.71**, which has an additional return of **$110,351.78** over just keeping your account in the Total Market Strategy, which you earned by logging into your TSP every so often to do some internal transfers—worth it, in my opinion!

Now, this is taking the very conservative route. The primary purpose of using these three arrows is to help you avoid large crashes, so you do not lose significant amounts of capital. Suppose you would like to use it to earn a higher rate of return than just waiting for the three green arrows to return. Then you can either guess the bottom of the downturn (super hard to do without a crystal ball), or you can tell yourself, "I will buy back in when the market goes down XX%." Historically, a significant market downturn goes down by 30% to 90%, so take your guess there. This is much riskier and not highly advised.

This can also be used on your brokerage account. Honestly, if you want to play it safe, I recommend the same allocation in your brokerage and do the same technical analysis to boost your return unless you want to try your hand at picking stocks and options. That is something that may have to wait for another book, or follow me at giwealthmanual.com for some additional training and insights.

Homework

What are your biggest takeaways from this chapter?

_____

_____

_____

Which TSP allocation fits your need the most?

_____

_____

_____

How much do you need to adjust your TSP on mypay.dfas. mil by to meet your goals?

_____

_____

Action Steps:

1. Decide how much % you will allocate from your paycheck (shoot for 5% minimum – full match, free money).
2. Adjust your mypay.dfas.mil to hit your % goal.
3. Select which allocation strategy you will use.
4. Log into TSP.gov to set your allocation strategy under the "Contribution Allocations." Type in the percentages you want to use under the fund of choice.
5. Decide if you want to use the Three Arrow Strategy.
6. Green arrows – Leave in Step 3 Allocation Strategy; Red Arrows move to 100% to G or F Fund (if interest rates are lower and not spiking).

CHAPTER 11

Investing How-To

Investing...how spooky and scary! Or at least that is what money managers want you to think so that you continue to pay the fees for them to manage YOUR money. But the funny thing is that countless studies have shown that nearly 96% of money managers have failed to beat the total stock market return. So, you pay them money to earn you money, but in the end, you lose more than what you could do yourself and they still get paid by you when your money plummets.

So, on average, the S&P 500 returns about 8% to 11% a year on average. You pay your money manager 0.5% to 2% a year of your portfolio amount to manage your money. So, if you have $50,000 being managed by a fund manager and make a 10% return in a year, $5,000, the fund manager will charge you up to a 2% fee at the end of the year, which equals $1,100. That may seem reasonable to you, but not to me. I'd rather save that $1,100 and manage my accounts myself, while the professional goes on and fails to beat the market by another

1% for others who chose to use them…Well, congrats, you just returned about 5.5% to 6% for the year. In the TSP chapter I showed you that you could do much better than that!

This event was very timely because when I was writing this chapter, a friend of mine asked me to analyze her new financial advisor's investment options. He charged a 1% fee annually on the total amount of money he managed (called AUM – Assets Under Management). I used the historical 10-year rate of return for the funds he outlined for her, and I did the same if you took another fund that you managed and mirrored the S&P 500, like the C Fund in TSP, to compare. This is how it faired:

Initial Investment $40,000 (no additional adds)
SPX (S&P 500 Index) after 10-Yrs: $115,744
Financial Advisor after 10-Yrs: $92,445

…$23,299 in fees and poor management. Wow! I would be pissed!

> *"If returns are going to 7 or 8 percent and you're paying 1 percent for fees, that makes an enormous difference in how much money you're going to have in retirement."*
>
> *– Warren Buffet*

Most money managers are more concerned about not losing money. Showing a loss of money is a tarnish on their records, and they will avoid that at all costs so that more of other people's money will come to them and they turn that money into more fees for their own paychecks. This includes financial planners, advisors, or mutual fund managers. So, what do we do?

Take responsibility for your own money. You can do so much better than 96% of the "professionals" out there. But it will take a little leg work on your end, but not much. And really, a lot of this information is going to come into play when you open your Roth IRA and your brokerage account—that is why I put this chapter after the TSP chapter.

The first step into investing is that you will need a brokerage for both an IRA and a traditional brokerage account.

What is a brokerage account?

How do you choose one? It all depends on what capabilities you need and the commissions involved (the cost of investing—this is how the brokerage makes money). Some will have a high commission and give you all the bells and whistles, a person to help you, etc. But honestly, we don't need all that at this point. We are just learning. So, we need the basics, a discount broker—one with low or free commissions and few bells and whistles. TDAmeritrade is my favorite bells and whistles discount broker, but Robinhood is a decent choice and is completely contained on your phone, which is probably #1 for beginners. But, at the time of this Robinhood does not offer IRAs (we will get into why this matters here in a little bit), so you will have to have other brokerages along with Robinhood. Your choice.

It is straightforward to set up. They will need your basic information—name, address, phone number, etc. They will also need your SSN for taxes and a bank account that you can link to your investing account for funding purposes. It shouldn't take longer than 10 to 15 mins to set up! I would open your Roth IRA and your brokerage account with the same institution to make it easy to track and to allow you to easily fund your Roth IRA with your brokerage account, if needed.

I know we talked about these different types of accounts, and I haven't explained them. So, let's do a quick down and dirty:

Traditional brokerage is a taxable account (any gains on your money are taxed) that allows you to buy and sell stocks and other investment vehicles. Keyword...taxed. There are no limits on how much you can deposit and withdraw at any time.

Traditional IRA – A tax-free (no taxes on gains) account that any money that you add to the account can be written off on your taxes (saves you money on taxes for that contribution year) and allows you to buy and sell the identical investment vehicles as the traditional brokerage account. It does have limits on how much you can deposit in a year, and if you withdraw before you retire, you will be fined.

Roth IRA is another tax-free account, but the money you add is already taxed money. So, it doesn't save you money today but saves you that money tomorrow. Why? I'll get into that next, but it has a contribution limit, and any money you earned in the account can't be taken out without a fine...keywording there that I will get into next, as well.

Traditional Brokerage vs. Traditional IRA vs. Roth IRA

First, let's do Traditional Brokerage vs. IRA; what are the pros and cons of each?

Traditional Brokerage

Pro

- No contribution limit—you can deposit as much money in a year as your little heart desires.
- Will not be penalized for withdrawing any of your funds from this account.
- Great for long-term and short-term investing and saving for financial goals.
- Not limited to what you can invest in.

Con

- Taxes...for the love of God, taxes...any returns that you make from your investments, you will have to claim on your tax return as additional income. (We will talk about how to lessen taxes in an upcoming investing section.)

IRA (Individual Retirement Account)

Pro

- Primarily used for retirement savings.
- Tax-advantaged...you will save on taxes by contributing to this fund.

Con

- You can only deposit a certain amount of money into the fund a year (2022: up to $6,000/yr, $7,000 if you are over 50 years of age).
- You will be penalized for withdrawing your money early (10% of the withdrawal amount), early being before 59 ½ years old.
- You are limited on some hazardous investment vehicles (ones I will never recommend someone doing, so I am not even going to let its name grace these pages).

But, if you are following this book, you will have both a traditional brokerage account and an IRA(s). But which?

Traditional IRA

Pro

- Tax savings today. Money that is deposited is claimed on your taxes and grows your tax return, lowering your current tax liability.

Con

- In retirement, you must pay taxes on all earned returns on your money.
- In retirement, you have RMD (required minimum distributions), so you MUST withdraw a specific amount (calculated by IRS worksheets) per year after the age of 72 (as of 2022).
- ANY withdrawal before retirement incurs a 10% penalty.

Roth IRA

<u>Pro</u>

- Tax savings tomorrow. In retirement, you get to withdraw all funds tax-free, including gains!
- Can withdraw only your deposited money at any time, penalty and tax-free, for example:

You are 50 years old. Since the age of 18, you have deposited $200K into your Roth, and you have earned $100K from growth (dividends, interest, and gains). You can withdraw the $200K penalty tax-free (almost like a savings account). But if you touch that $100K of growth, you will be charged a 10% penalty.

- In retirement, you do not have any RMD; keep growing that money.

<u>Con</u>

- Do not get to claim deposited money on your tax return.
- As of 2022, if your total income is more significant than $129K for single or $204K for married, you cannot contribute to a Roth IRA.

Rule of Thumb – Do a Roth IRA if your taxes are lower today than what they will be at retirement age (90% of us), and do a Traditional IRA for the opposite. But the Roth is an AMAZING deal!

Those are the main ones that 95% of you will encounter. There are some special ones, and if you think you qualify, I would talk to a CPA to help you in that area because I fall in that 95% bucket that has never needed them…sorry.

Another thing that you will encounter when setting up your accounts is "margin."

Margin – money borrowed from a broker to purchase an investment. It will amplify both gains and **losses**. *– Investopedia, 2022*

For the love of God! DO NOT touch and apply for margin when you are starting. I learned this the hard way when I first started investing…just don't. In the future, you may decide to go this route, but for now, your investing life will be a whole lot simpler if you avoid it.

Ok, cool, you have your account set up. From this point on, this applies to both your IRAs and brokerage accounts. So, what is next? You must fund your account—it needs to have money to invest. This is where that linked bank account comes in handy. Some brokerage accounts require a minimum (I've seen $1K to $3K) initial deposit to begin. Some also count a monthly direct deposit that will work in order to open the account…it all depends on the company; it will say when you sign up! So, get that money in there. You may need to save up the money from your budget for a few months to get the initial deposit amount, and that is A-OK! Once you get the initial deposit set, set up automatic deposits based on your budget. If you can do this on your LES through automatic allocations—even better! The less you think about it, the more automatic it will be.

You have money in your account; now, the moment we have all been waiting for…purchasing your first investment! There are multiple directions that you can go:

Stocks – is a fractional piece of a publicly-traded company. If you own a company's stock, you own a part of that company. – Investopedia, 2022

Mutual Funds – A mutual fund is a financial vehicle made up of a pool of money collected from many investors to invest in securities like stocks, bonds, and other assets. Mutual funds are operated by professional money managers, who allocate the fund's investments and attempt to produce gains or income for the fund's investors. – Investopedia, 2022

Electronically Traded Funds (ETF) – is a type of pooled investment security that operates much like a mutual fund. ETFs will track a particular index, sector, commodity, or asset, but unlike mutual funds, ETFs can be purchased or sold on a stock exchange the same way a regular stock can. – Investopedia, 2022

Bonds are a "fixed-income" (does not move much) instrument representing a loan made by an investor to a borrower, typically a corporation or government. – Investopedia, 2022

Index Funds – is a type of ETF with a portfolio constructed to match or track the components of a financial market index, such as the S&P 500 or the Dow Jones Industrial Average. – Investopedia, 2022

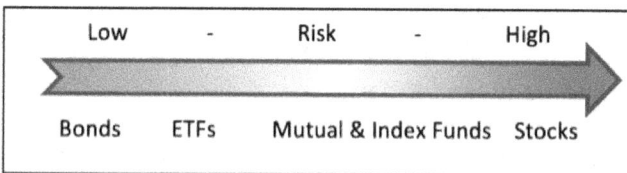

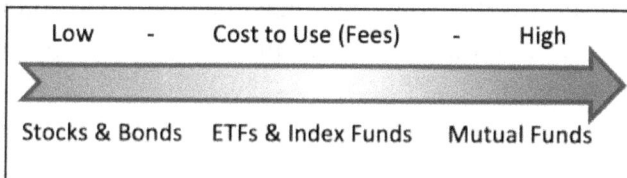

Low	-	Risk	-	High
Bonds	ETFs	Mutual & Index Funds		Stocks

Low	-	Cost to Use (Fees)	-	High
Stocks & Bonds		ETFs & Index Funds		Mutual Funds

Stocks will be your highest risk investment but your cheapest investment because you manage it yourself, so the cost is just your time that you are spending to research companies or on commissions. Today, commission-free stock investing is more common than not., so win-win! ETFs are your next highest risk investment due to their ability to trade like a stock. You can find some very high-risk and low-risk ETFs, so it is a mixed bag. But, an ETF is still like a mutual fund—someone manages it behind the scene, so you have a fraction of a percentage that is taken out of your account as a fee in order to invest with the ETF, just not to the level of mutual funds. Mutual funds are the middle of the road for returns. (You can find low-risk and high-risk mutual funds, just like ETFs.) But mutual funds are managed by a well-paid person daily, and with that comes high fees. So, it is the most expensive option! Bonds will be your lowest risk possible and are cheap to own, just like owning an ETF. But, while I say costly, it is only a couple %; there are ETFs as low as .03% and mutual funds as high as 2% to 3%! That's a lot to spend on a $100K portfolio per year—$3K per $100K per year...and that is even if it loses you money!

It is not just about the reward or the investment risk; you must also think about the cost of owning the asset—a little piece that many tend to forget.

So, the next part we cover will match your risk tolerance and the type of investor you would like to become. Do you want to be a basic, moderate, or advanced investor? Let's break that down next.

Basic Investor

This is the simplest form…which is what basic tends to mean, so hey! This type of investor would like a "set-it-and-forget-it" or hands-off investment style. Or one who has a lower risk tolerance (can't afford financially or emotionally to lose their money), whether this is due to age or just lifestyle. It doesn't matter. Here is what you need to do:

Date of Completion	Activity
	Identify your left over from your budget—this is the amount you can put in this account
	Save $3,000 in a savings account to meet the minimum investment amount required
	Open a "General Investing" account with Vanguard* (investor.vanguard.com)
	Transfer the saved $3,000 to your Vanguard account
	Invest fully in the Vanguard Total Stock Market Index Fund (Ticker: VTSAX)
	Add more money when your budget allows. Invest in VTSAX with that additional, rinse and repeat. With VTSAX, you can set up auto-investing through Vanguard coupled with auto-deposit from your LES, and you will be 100% hands-free

Date of Completion	Activity
	Change your account to DRIP –Dividend Reinvestment Program**
	Let it work—if you have a hard time with emotions around bad stock days, NEVER check your account. You can check it when you are about to retire

* Why Vanguard? It is an excellent brokerage account with unbeatable fees on its investment options. They are nearly unmatched. Very basic, though, not the best for moderate or advanced investors.

** DRIP? Dividend Reinvestment Program: When you earn a dividend, the program automatically reinvests the payout back into the investment vs. going to your cash account and making nothing.

This method of investing falls under the term "Dollar Cost Averaging." Also known as DCA. A straightforward concept and one that is used all around the globe. But, most use it like fucking morons, because they are uneducated on how to invest. Not YOU! Because you are getting your education from this book on how to use DCA properly!

> *"If you like spending six to eight hours per week working on investments, do it. If you don't, then dollar-cost average into Index Funds."*
>
> *Warren Buffett*

While I don't 100% agree with the above quote (it doesn't take six to eight hours a week to invest), it does highlight a great point. If you don't want to invest too much time in an activity, find the easiest way to do it, the same with investing. And DCA is the easiest way to do it.

The definition of DCA from Investopedia is "the practice of systematically investing equal amounts, spaced out over regular intervals, regardless of price." What this does is "smooths" out the upward and downward swings in the market. Think of your TSP; it pulls money from your account every paycheck and buys into your chosen fund without considering the price.

You do the same in this style of investing. Commit to supporting $X to your Vanguard or other accounts per month, have it auto-invest into VTSAX, and let it ride! Easy-peasy.

Note: If you get a large bonus, say a reenlistment bonus, you want to invest all of that in your brokerage account. Invest that as one large lump sum. It is better to have the whole pot of money working for you than slowly adding it $1,000 at a time over X number of years.

Moderate Investor

We will utilize more stocks in our portfolio for the moderate investor to yield a more significant return each year. So, with more risk taken, the higher the reward you may receive. And this is going to take a little more work on your part. So, again, if you would rather have a hands-off investment style, you don't need to read this section or the next.

You can do this highest risk/highest return by focusing your portfolio all in stocks, or lowering that risk by doing a percentage of stocks and the basic investor style (finding a low fee index fund/ETF such as that mentioned in the basic investor section).

Example – High Risk	Example – Moderate Risk
90% to 100% Stocks (10–20)	30% to 40% VTI* Fund
0% to 10% Cash**	40% to 50% Stocks (5–10)
	0% to 10% Cash**

I recommend VTI here because you will actively manage it. VTSAX in "Basic Investors" has about .01% higher fees, but you can auto-invest with that one. (The broker automatically invests your money for you.) Vanguard does not allow you to do that with VTI, which is the difference. If you want hands-off for that portion of your fund, do VTSAX.

**Why the hell do we need cash? – For greater returns, that is why!*

Why is cash necessary? "Most millionaires are made in a recession (large market crash)." Having cash in reserves allows you to buy great companies going through a downturn for REALLY cheap. Once they rebound, your rates of return skyrocket!

I recommend using the red/green arrows outlined in the TSP section to decide how much cash you should hold. If green arrows are continuing, don't worry much about cash, you can hold as little as 0%, if you choose to. As you start seeing red arrows turn on, begin transitioning to as much as 30% to 40% cash by selling portions of winning stocks (that you have held over one year or more) so you can buy them cheaper when prices drop. Or you can go to 100% cash if you are feeling feisty…but remember, the arrows are not foolproof, so they may turn around to green without you buying any new stocks. The choice is yours, but their track record is quite high.

We derailed there, chasing squirrels over here. Two other questions come out of that tangent above. Which stocks? Where do you buy them? Where do you sell them?

Choosing Stocks

Let's start simple…ask yourself these four questions:

1. Does the stock (company) make the world a better place by being around?
    a. I.e., does this company make our lives easier, bring us closer, and improve the world around us?

2. Is this stock (company) the absolute best in what it does among its competitors?
    a. I.e., think Apple vs. Blackberry. Apple is the top premium cell phone and computer company—and people are willing to pay those prices because they are good at what they do.

3. Will this stock be around in the next three to five years and have a higher price than today?

4. Does this stock (company) promote my life values, and do I want to support them with my money?
   a. I.e., if you are against smoking, why would you invest in a company that produces cigarettes?

If you can't answer "Yes" to each of those questions when looking at a company, you are looking at the wrong company. This is because you need to be 100% certain that you believe in the company—even if it falls 50% in market cash...you won't be worried that it will go bankrupt and lose your money. And...if you followed my advice, you would be comfortable pouring more money in at those low prices! Win-win!

One thing, though, that I want to cover really quickly is how much stock and how many different companies you should buy. Since this kind of stock picking is pretty surface-level, you carry some risk that the company you pick can go tits up at a moment's notice due to shitty management. So, to minimize this risk, you want to own multiple companies (if you can, depending on your total amount of money in your account). We will go over this a little more here in a couple of sections.

Things to keep in mind:
- DO NOT own more than 20% of your stock account (total account is $10,000...max $1,000 per stock/company).
- ONLY invest in companies you know and understand...Buffet calls this "Investing only within your Circle of Competence." Case in point, I know nothing about healthcare, so I will never invest in healthcare!

Buy Points

I mean, buying can be easy as shit if you just do it willy-nilly. Which some people do...psst, it isn't helping them much, mainly by allowing them to liquidate all of their accounts in losses. There are two things to think about here when deciding on a buy point, or entry point as it is sometimes called. Does the current market condition support a buy? (AKA, is the market about to shit the bed and drop 50%?...watch those arrows!) and is this an excellent price to buy at—what is a reasonable price?

Let's hit the first question—good market conditions for a buy. And no, I am not talking about "timing the market," where you wait to find the best deal to buy or sell because you feel you know best. Well, buddy, you don't. The stock market is fueled by emotion: the emotions of fear and greed. Stocks drop when people become fearful of what is to come, and rise when people become greedy for prospects. So, if you think that your singular emotional brain can outguess billions of others...then you need to unfuck yourself and get your ego in check. BUT! We can use that to our advantage!

> *"Be Fearful when others are Greedy, and Greedy when others are Fearful."*
>
> *– Warren Buffet*

So, the stock market is just a GIANT class in human psychology. It can be fascinating when you view it from this angle. So, how do we use this to our advantage? We go against the herd, that is how. When others are panicking, we remain calm. (Therefore, we need to have a comfort with the companies that we invest in.) We do this by keeping the following in mind...the GI Wealth Analysis Pentagon (...see what I did there!) because it is all based on proper analysis.

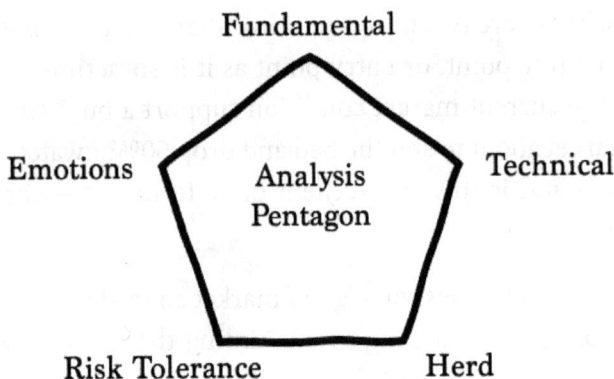

Fundamental

Emotions

Analysis Pentagon

Technical

Risk Tolerance   **Herd**

Fundamental Analysis

Fundamentals are based more on actual numbers and reports. Fundamental markers include the company's health, the debt load, the stock price compared with the industry that the company competes in, etc. While it doesn't give you a set direction for the company, combined with the other four indicators it ensures that you are on a healthy path to success in the market. These are the areas that we need to focus on in the fundamental area:

- Is the company the "King" in what they do? Think Amazon for e-commerce, Apple for high-end electronics, or Coca-Cola for beverages. Why? Because they have a higher chance of being around for the next five to ten years—we know there will be loyal customers to the brand.

- Are there any events happening in the world or in the industry that will plummet their stock price? Examples include wars, stock market uncertainty, e-coli outbreak at a fast-food restaurant, etc.

- Is the company well run? Is the company doing good for the world? Is it carrying a large amount of debt which could cause bankruptcy during a recession?

Many websites can help you with this, including your free access to Morningstar through your branch's library. If you want to take an easy way out, pull up Morningstar and read the analyst's view on the company. (If there is no analyst report, then it probably isn't an industry king—that's a good giveaway.) But that report will give you a fantastic insight into the company.

Another great site to look at is stockcard.io; it puts everything you need to know into a great green, amber, and red quad-chart. Something after any Army Joe's heart! Sign up for a free account and search for a company you are interested in. You can also do a "stock screener," aka, a filtered search. If you go this route, you want to search with the following filters:

- Market Cap* (Medium & Large Cap)
- Company Strength (Green)
- Sales Growth (Green)
- Cash Availability (Green)
- Management Effectiveness (Green)
- Profitability (Green)

Market Capitalization (cap) –represents a company's market "value." Market cap fluctuates with the stock price, because it is equated by multiplying the current stock price by the number of shares available to buy. It is a measure of how large or small a company is. The smaller the market cap, the more volatile and riskier it is; the larger the market cap, the less risky. –Investopedia, 2022

Score this list of companies and compare it with Morningstar's analyst views. You should come out at the other end and see if you understand the company, if they live up to your values and if it is a company that you want to be an owner in!

Just remember, do not invest in any company that you are not willing to hold it for 10+ years…you don't really have to do that, but you should have that mindset when investing! My recommendation would be to find ten "core" stocks to make up your portfolio. These ten stocks are ones that you personally value and cannot live without. They are fully in your wheelhouse of understanding and you know them inside and out. These ten have a constant presence in your account and any stocks outside these ten are lesser known, but still great companies.

You will more than likely not be invested in all ten at one time, unless we are coming out of a recession when everything is on sale. If that is the case, fill your portfolio up with your core companies, get all that you can at cheaper and cheaper prices. We will show you in the following sections how to do this.

Technical Analysis

Technical analysis is a measurement of psychology. It is looking at stock charts to indicate the direction of a stock price, how quickly it moves and for how long (momentum), and most importantly, levels where other investors are buying and selling! We have already explored the first few in the TSP section with the arrows! Remember, the three arrows show where the stock market is moving, or it's showing that large institutional investors (hedge fund, mutual fund managers, etc.) are moving in and out of the stock, and if the stock is overbought or oversold. All essential things to know. And all three together indicate a significant market shift! A shift from bearish to bullish indicated when you should be selling winning positions and when you should be loading up on cash in your account! Simple!

There is so much more that you can do with technical analysis, but for this strategy and to get you started, this is really all you need to know.

Herd

Remember, we want to see what the "herd" or most other investors are doing, and do the complete opposite…in most cases! There are times when we can use them to our advantage.

When the market is crashing (red arrows), do the opposite of the herd. They will be rapidly selling because they think the sky is falling. BUT, since we are wise, we don't let our emotions get the better of us. We know that this is a great company, and we sit tight and buy more when we can.

But, when we are in a bull market (green arrows), we can use the herd mentality to our advantage. The age of the internet makes this so much easier, and you have an additional perk of being in the military because of what your branch's library provides. There are three websites that I urge you to look at when searching for where the herd mentality is—Morningstar. com, Seekingalpha.com, and Dataroma.com. You already get premium Morningstar through the military (search on your military's portal or library). And Seeking Alpha, you don't need a premium account either (plus it is crazy expensive).

Morningstar is an excellent website for fundamental and herd analysis to analyze funds and companies! We've already touched on fundamentals, but for the herd, it is great to look at the analyst section to see their research and their general feeling of the stock in question. As a member of the military, you are entitled to premium membership; you have free access to this! Score! Also, their 1 to 5-star rating is good to see if it is expensive or cheap (in their eyes). If it is already a 1-star company, it might not have additional room to run up and, therefore limited profit, but that is something we will look at shortly.

For your information, on Morningstar, their star rating is based off of their fair value calculation, 1-star being way overpriced and 5-star being way underpriced.

Seeking Alpha is more of a chat room/forum where professional analysts and…well, not-so-professional analysts can write articles about individual stocks or the market as a whole. It is an expensive website to be a premium member of, and premium members get to view all the articles. As a free member, you don't get to read the articles, but if you are on a computer (which doesn't work on the app) or the browser on your phone, you get to see if the articles are "bullish," "bearish," or "neutral." And that is all we need. If most articles are bearish, it may be an excellent time to buy; if bullish, it is a perfect time to think about selling. If neutral, we may need to do additional research. This may seem backwards, but if we found our wonderful company through our research, we WANT to buy when others are selling and the price is dropping! "And when are people are" jacking up the price with their greed, it might be time to punch the cash register.

Dataroma is a treasure trove of information and a straightforward website. It gives information on "Super-investors" and "Insiders." A super-investor has a hedge fund with millions and billions of assets under management (AUM). They must report what they buy and sell in those funds quarterly (four times a year). Here we can look at what they are buying and what they paid. Warren Buffet is one of those who must report; he knows what to buy! Why not use our resources wisely and cheat off their paper? Insiders are the management figures (CEO, CFO, etc.) in large companies—they must report when they invest in the company they own and/or work for. If many insiders are buying, it may mean that it is a good time to buy at an excellent price. If they are all selling…well, do I need to say it?

> *"I just wanted to clone what Buffet did…"*
>
> – *Mohnish Pabrai*

Use others' knowledge to benefit you; don't try to outsmart the masses! That is why this is a critical concept in the Analysis Pentagon.

Quick note: Once you do your herd analysis, turn off the damn news...the news's primary goal is to stir the pot and cause anxiety and fear, so more viewers turn to them. This also includes Subreddits and others that are pure doom and gloom. The news will cause you to doubt your abilities faster than anything else and make you sell when you shouldn't. Turn it off! Plus, you will be a happier person in general if you do...but this isn't a happiness self-help book.

Risk Tolerance

> "Risk comes from not knowing what you are doing...never invest in a business you cannot understand."
>
> – Warren Buffet

Risk tolerance, is this stock too risky for you? Or is it just right? How do you know if it is too risky? Look at the stock chart. Does it move up and down wildly? Does it carry much debt? Is it a cutting-edge company, inventing new things, pressing the boundaries of what is already on the market? Those will be your highest risk companies (think and look at Tesla – Ticker: TSLA). Can you stomach those crazy movements? No? Look for a company with both their feet on the ground...and yes, pun fully intended on that one—you are welcome!

Within risk tolerance, you must also "size" it to your portfolio. By this I mean, how much of this company do you want to fill your portfolio (0% to 10% of your total account $)? If you are not 100% sure that it will be bigger and stronger in the next three to five years, don't give it 10% of your money!

A great way to tell how risky a stock may be is to look at the "Beta," you can find this on most stock information websites. Beta shows how volatile a stock is compared to the S&P500. Now, this depends on your timeline to retirement, but for someone who has longer than 5-8 years until retirement. A beta of 1.0 means it is as volatile as the S&P500, which is a medium-low risk. Below a 1.0 is low risk. 1.2-1.5 is medium risk. 1.5-2.0 is a medium-high risk. And 2.0 is a high-risk stock!"

The riskier the stock, the less you should invest because these have the highest chance to go bankrupt...that means going to $0...and that would suck—we don't want that suckage.

Emotions

When I am talking about emotions, this is your final check before purchase; this is a check on YOUR feelings. Are you 100% comfortable with this company? If this company drops 50% tomorrow, are you going to panic sell, or will you be excited that it is cheaper and you can buy more shares for less? Hint, it should be the latter. Are you confident that the fundamentals point out that this company will not go bankrupt? Are you ready to pull the trigger?

> *"If you cannot control your emotions, you cannot control your money."*
>
> *– Warren Buffett*

Yes to all? Then let's pull that trigger!

Buying

Buying is not the first step—research is the first step. Before we buy, again, we must be 100% comfortable owning this company's stock for the next three to five years. Can you enthusiastically say that you are excited? Awesome. Then let us proceed to buy.

Most people think that you make your money when you sell your stock. In fact, you make your money when you purchase. The level you buy at sets the potential profit for when you get around to selling. So, to ensure a great profit (a significant profit is above the average market return of about 8%—there is no point doing this if we can't beat the market), we need to purchase a stock at a level where we have a great chance of making a profit, and we can do this by studying key psychological levels of the price chart.

Whoa, whoa. Psychological levels? What the hell are you talking about, Ian? I know, it sounds pretty "new age-y." But remember, I said earlier that the stock market is just a giant study in psychology? We can see that in the daily stock price—fear and greed.

You don't need a degree; you just need to be shown what to look for. So, let me paint a picture and explain what we are looking at. This is where technical analysis comes into play! Look at the following chart:

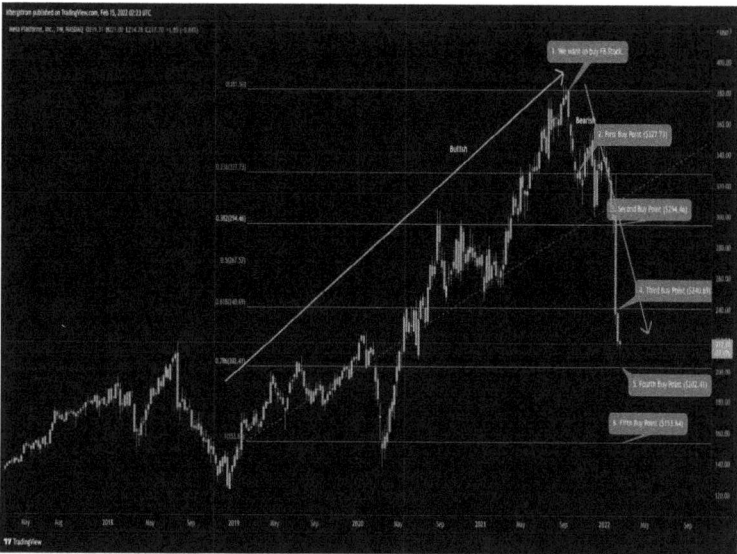

Ok, so what the hell is going on in this chart? Well, many things…and they aren't as complicated as they first appear.

First of all, I am sure most of you are used to seeing a stock chart with a single line that waves back and forth. That is basic, which isn't bad—it can remove much confusion. But, if you are serious about improving your investing skills, I would get used to this view. And this view is called "candle-stick" charting. Because, hey, they look like little candles with their cute lil wicks. Let's break it down:

Increasing :
Bullish Candle Stick

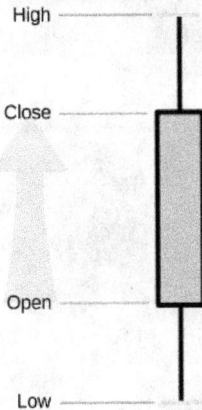

High ————

Close ————

Open ————

Low ————

Decreasing :
Bearish Candle Stick

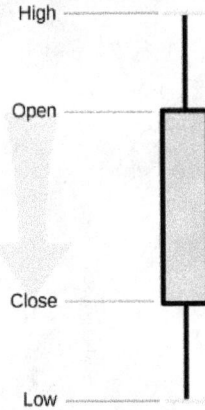

High ————

Open ————

Close ————

Low ————

* Courtesy of R-Blogger.com

The top of the top wick, labeled "high," is the highest price that stock reached during a given period (minute, hour, day, week, month, year, etc.). The "close" was the price when the market closed (1600 EST on non-holidays). The "open" is the price when the market opens (0930 EST on non-holidays). And finally, the low is the lowest the price reached during the given period. Simple! Now, why is one green and one red? What the hell is bearish and bullish?

Green means that the "close" price was HIGHER than the "open" price, which means that the stock's price increased during the period. And the code for that is "bullish" period. Why bullish? No clue. But the best way that I remember this is when a bull attacks something, he dips his head and swipes upwards!

Red means that the "close" price was LOWER than the "open" price, meaning that the stock's price decreased during the period. The code for this movement is "bearish." When a bear attacks something, he raises his paw over his head and swipes <u>down</u>!

The last thing to know is how large the "body" or the candle part is and how long the "wicks" are. The body and wick show how much movement in the price there was in a given period. While this is not very important when it comes to our investing style, it is a good thing to know, as they can indicate some coming change in direction or the psychology of the market. Large, long candles can indicate a lot of fear (red) or greed (green). Small candles could mean confusion, or that you are around a key psychological level—what the hell do we mean by that?

Key psychological levels equal Fibonacci levels. Let's go back to history and math class. Fibonacci was an Italian mathematician back in the 13th century who devised a formula used to calculate the growth of rabbit populations. It was realized that this was a constant formula within biology, the swirl in a nautilus shell, the branching of trees, and the spiral of a pineapple. It is referred to as the Fibonacci numbers, golden ratio, and Fibonacci spiral. Once turned into ratios (percentages between key numbers), technical analysts noticed that these ratios match up with key psychological levels within stock price charts. The levels are where the stock price tends to stall or reverse. If you refer to the stock chart image on page 142, your Fibonacci lines or "Retracements" are the colorful lines at 78.6%, 61.8%, 50%,

38.2%, and 23.6%. They are drawn between a high and a low point on a chart. How?

> Step 1: Find the stock you want to analyze and change it to a weekly, five-year chart.
>
> Step 2: Find the lowest point in the last two to three years.
>
> Step 3: Select your "Fibonacci Retracements." Click on the lowest point and drag up to your most current high point.
>
> Step 4: You may need to adjust your chart to match up periods of "sideways movement," or a large grouping of candles that start or stop at a relatively consistent level.
>
> Step 5: It is not a perfect science; it is more of an art. See what looks best to you, and get better the more you practice.

How do we use this now? We use these Fibonacci levels to indicate our buy points and as we will see in the next section, our sell points.

So, with the chart image of the ticker symbol "FB," which is the old Facebook, or now Meta Platforms, on page 142a, the scenario is as follows:

We identify at the beginning of September 2022 that we want to invest in FB. It is at the highest price we have ever seen for the stock, so we know it is not the proper time to buy. So, we draw our Fibonacci levels to identify what times are actually best.

Our first level is the 23.6% level, about $328.

We have a total account balance of $20,000, and we want to invest in 10 stocks—so that leaves us $2,000 per stock! We don't want to buy $2,000 in stocks in the first purchase. We want to break it into four to five segments or "tranches." This allows us to lower our "cost basis" (our average purchase price), giving us a higher return when we sell. So, if we do five tranches, that leaves us $400 per purchase.

Our first purchase is at $328, which is one share.

Our second purchase is at $290.50, which is one share.

The stock price drops like crazy, and we get a third buy price at the 61.8% level for $240*, which is one more share.

> *Note, if you want to be more hands-off, you can set "Buy Limit Orders" with your brokerage account, automatically purchasing our shares at the level price level that we want to buy. So, in this case, we would set buy limit orders at each of our Fibonacci levels ahead of time. This would make our third purchase at a 50% level for $268. It depends on if you want hands-on or hands-off investing.

Our fourth will potentially be at $202, two shares!

Our fifth and final will potentially be at $154, three shares!

This gives us an average of eight shares at $215.56! So, we make a profit when the stock price climbs back above $216 if it drops below our fifth buy price! This is the power of cost basis averaging!

This is why it is SO important to be confident in what you are doing and what company you are investing in. Can you imagine going through that? It is super scary to hold on and continue to buy more as the herd is abandoning ship and TV investing personalities are screaming "SELL!"

What we are doing here is called "Value Investing." We are finding good companies at low prices. It isn't fashionable or high-paced; it involves tuning out your friends and your Uncle Phil with that hot stock tip he heard about at work. And it consists of A LOT of patience. You need to WAIT for your stock to drop to your buy points, which can be tedious at first. But man, when that price drops, it gets super exciting quickly!

Note: This will take more patience but can increase your returns by lowering your cost basis. Identify the companies you like and wait for the "Red Arrows" on the Russell 2000 (RUT) index. Start your buying levels once the RUT has three red arrows—you won't be buying stocks as often with this strategy, but you will have a better return.

Ok, you found your company and placed all four to five of your buy limit orders. Congrats! Now what? It is time to stay off the news and out of your account! Check your accounts once every two weeks to see if there are any other good companies to buy, or time to set sell orders—that is the next topic. The more you stay out of your account, the better. When stocks are dropping (perfect buying environment), you will see A LOT of red in your account. And yes, that is scary—the red color spikes something in our psychology to be scared. This will bring on doubt and cause you to think that this is the end of the US government as we know it...which won't be the case...and if it is, your investment accounts won't matter much!

Don't trigger panic selling when others are, by staying out of the herd. And don't trigger panic buying when others say you are missing out! Do your research and gain your confidence within your specific risk tolerance and you will be golden and prosperous!

So, great, you did all that and your stocks are up 20 to 100%+. But, how do we know when to take profit by selling and investing in other depressed companies? Let's go over that next.

Selling

> *"Calling someone who trades actively in the market an investor is like calling someone who repeatedly engages in one-night stands a romantic...the stock market is designed to transfer money from the active to the patient."*
>
> *– Warren Buffet*

Ok, so we have bought all the tranches that we could get. Sometimes all five of your tranches do not go through, which is ok. The market tends to crash every eight to twelve years, so there will be multiple times in your life when you will get some fantastic downturns that will give you excellent returns! More millionaires are made when the market crashes or a recession occurs because they buy great companies cheap!

But I digress, selling is easier than buying, except for one thing...and that is taxes. Damn taxes...why do I need to bring up taxes? Because how long you hold (time that has elapsed between when you buy and sell) will determine the amount you will be taxed on your profit.

Capital Gains Tax

> Note: This only applies to your taxed accounts, your traditional brokerage accounts, and not your IRAs.

According to Investopedia (2022), capital gains tax "is the levy on the profit from an investment incurred when an investment is sold, which is applied to stocks, bonds, jewelry, coin collections, and real estate." There are two types of capital gains tax: long-term and short-term—it all revolves around a year.

Capital Gains = Sell Price – Buy Price

Short-term capital gains tax is applied to any investment that has been held for less than one year. These tax rates can change year to year, but they are based on your regular income tax rate. The rates range from 10% to 37% of the profit if you earn over ~$500K per year and are single, and over ~$600K if you are married.

Long-term capital gains tax is applied to any investment that has been held for more than one year. Again, the rate changes year-to-year, but it is less impactful on your profit if you hold over a year. It ranges from 0% to 20%, that is it! A huge incentive to keep your investments over a year!

So, let's say you make an income of $70K per year and are single. You made $5,000 in your taxed brokerage account. If you held for less than a year, you would be taxed 22% ($1,100 in taxes). If you held that for more than a year and earned the same profit, it would be taxed at 15% ($750 in taxes). It's a small saving at this level, but is impactful when you have an income over $500K per year as it's a difference in the short-term of 35% to 37%, and long-term 20%!

In short, with value investing we don't want to sell amazing companies if they continue to remain excellent, but at the minimum we want to hold for three to five years. Unless the price skyrockets, let's look at another option that I call the 50/50 rule.

50/50 Rule

Again, with this strategy we are holding for a minimum of one year, no matter what. It is simple. When you have a profit of 50% (say you bought company WTF's stock for $100, and it shoots up to $150 in a year, that is a 50% gain—multiply the price you bought it for by "1.5"), sell 50% of the stock you own. This does two things: First, it locks in your 50% profit score and second, it frees up cash to buy into another excellent stock that is dropping to do it again. Score-score!

For the rest of the 50% of your stock, you can either shoot for another 50%, a total of 100% (hard to do), and hold it forever, or investigate the next section for my other strategy.

Now, my advice would be to do this 50/50 strategy for smaller accounts (less than $50K). This is so you can free up money to better diversify your account by buying different stocks in your account, just in case we missed something in our research and the company is a dud. It happens—some investments can look like a pretty penny, but the CEO is doing something evil behind the scenes that he is not sharing with us, and it goes bankrupt. It is always a possibility. So, take half of your winnings and branch out to other great companies!

Fibonacci of Selling

I would use this strategy for your leftover 50% that you did not sell in the small account strategy. Or if you have over $50K, you can easily invest in 10 to 20 companies!

We used Fibonacci Retracements to indicate where we should buy. We can use Fibonacci Retracements to indicate sell levels. Some programs that you can use to draw stock charts call it "Fibonacci Extensions." But it is straightforward. All it takes is taking your Fibonacci Retracement that you already drew to find your buy levels, duplicate or copy that image, take the reproduced photo, drag that new 0% line, and overlay it on your old 100% line like a hat. This will extend your Fibonacci lines and double them to give "future levels." See below:

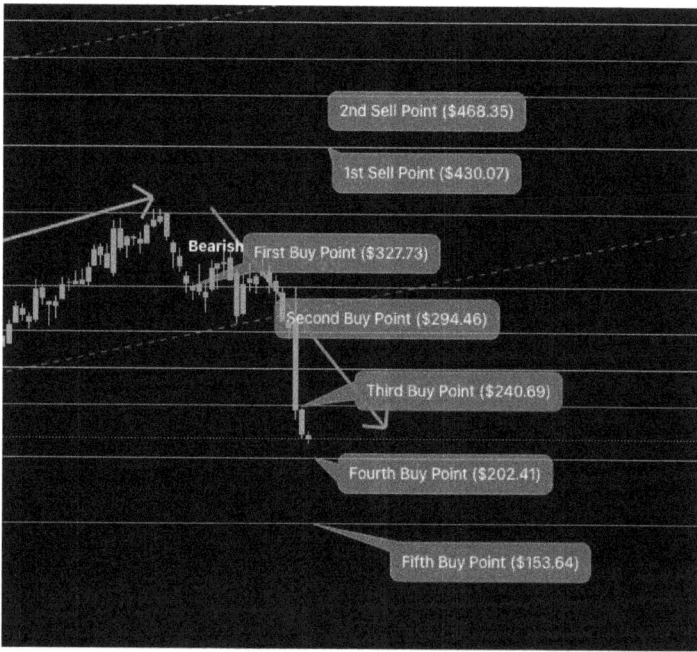

You will make two sell points, one at the first Fibonacci line above the old 100% line, and the second at the second line above the new 0% line, which is also the old 100% line. Suppose we pull down our example from before in the buy section.

Buy Cost Basis: 8 Shares at $215.56

Sell #1: 4 Shares at $430.07 Profit: $858.04 ROI*: 99.5%
Sell #2: 4 Shares at $468.35 Profit: $1,011.16 ROI: 117%
*Reminder: RO I – Return on Investment

The final profit is $1,869.20 and an ROI of 108%. If that takes five years to do, it is still a return of 21.6% per year! A lot better than what a fund manager or the S&P 500 will give you at an average of 8% per year.

It is time to take that extra cash you made and invest it back into another great company!

My last word of advice is pay attention to the red arrows; if green arrows start changing over to red, and you have been in your stocks for more than a year with a good return (greater than 20%), I would begin selling. This allows you to capture profits before the market plummets, which will enable you to have a bunch of cash to buy even cheaper companies when the market as a whole plummets. Win, flippin' win!

But that is about it when it comes to improving your investing life! Again, it is not for everyone, but if you want to have more control over your financial life and the gain it can give you, this is one of the best strategies for most individuals! Now, go out there and make some money!

Tip: Some brokerage accounts allow you to have "paper money" accounts. This account has fake money but will enable you to simulate investing. So, if you still feel uneasy, practice in a paper money account for a year or so until you are comfortable!

Advanced Investor

There is soooo much more you could do in the investment world to create a more significant return on your money. This is something that I have spent five years perfecting and have gained some fantastic guidance from a couple of mentors who helped me balloon my accounts, going from $700 to

$180K in just under 2 years! But I want to apologize ahead of time—if I include how I did this, it would turn this book into a dictionary-sized novel. What is included is understanding great companies at a deeper level, how to correctly price companies to get the most significant ROI possible, and how to use options to balloon your returns safely. So, please, head on over to my website at go.giwealthmanual.com/masterclass and learn more about becoming an advanced investor.

Homework

What are your biggest takeaways from this chapter?

_____

_____

_____

_____

_____

What type of investor are you?

_____

_____

What are your next steps based on your investor type?

_____

_____

What are your 10 core companies?

_____

_____

_____

Investing Flow

* Do not move on to the next step until you finish this first:

1. 5% to TSP

2. Max out Roth IRA

3a. Early Retirement: Invest rest into brokerage

3b. Retire at 60: Max out TSP

4a. Early Retirement: Continue step 3a

4b. Retire at 60: Invest in brokerage

*If it brings you more comfort, build up your three to six-month high-yield savings account for loss of income fund between steps 2 and 3. All debt also needs to be paid off before moving to step 3.

CHAPTER 12

Prepping for Post-Military

There is one thing that is guaranteed within our military career, and this is that we are all going to leave the military at some point, whether that is by our choice, our bodies breaking down, or we just fucked up. We may leave before 20 years, at 20 years, or long after. It doesn't matter…what matters is that we *will* leave the military. So, before we do, let's protect ourselves and set ourselves up the best we can for our post-military lives. We can either have some minor inconvenience for an excellent future or do no work now and struggle to make up later.

But I know you will pick the first choice because you picked up this book. Because by reading this book and getting to this chapter, you already chose a minor inconvenience to better yourself for the future. So, props—good job for securing your own way!

Step 1: Become Financially Literate

Here we are, back at financial literacy, and oddly enough, we are close to the end of this book! I hope this book has been an incredible journey for you and has allowed you to feel and become more financially literate. By picking up and finishing this book, you have done way more than most of your peers. You should be proud of yourself!

But you can take this journey a lot farther! There are so many other books, courses, rabbit holes, etc., that you can go down and learn from. So, I challenge you not to stop learning about and growing your finances and life. Visit my website; I will have a "library" of books that I have read, put into positive action, and that I recommend. All this can help you grow financially!

So, excellent job for already completing step 1!

Step 2: Utilize and Document Your Free Medical Care

I will be honest...I sucked at this. When I was on Active Duty, I had the shitty mindset of "ahh...yeah, my knee hurts, I'll suck it up, I don't want to burden the doctor." Holy shit, if I could go back and slap myself around for saying that, I would! That is why the doctor is there—we have free health care, dumbass self. USE IT!

And really, what I am talking about is your Veteran Affair (VA) disability compensation. Which, in essence, is tax-free, again; TAX-FREE, payments for the rest of your life, monthly—for all the fucked-up things that the military put you through! Most of us come out of the military beaten up and broken, whether mentally or physically. And while I hope no one has to be mentally and physically broken, we need to face facts here and claim what is ours.

Back to where I went wrong. The first time I sat down with my VA representative while he was looking at my medical records, it went something like this:

VA Guy: "How long did you say you were in?"

Me: "About 10.5 years."

VA Guy: "Oh…I normally see medical records about three times this long for someone in 10 years."

Cue Morgan Freeman voice…"And this is when Ian knew he'd fucked up."

I didn't want to be a burden on my doctor, so I didn't see him for my minor injuries. I just sucked them up and did my own thing! The thing with this is…you NEED medical proof to be able to claim a disability. And the longer the rap sheet of that injury, the stronger your claim is!

Go to the damn doctors! When your back hurts, schedule an appointment! Get a referral for a massage if you can! If your toe hurts during running, schedule an appointment! If you have acid reflux, don't pop a bunch of TUMS, get seen for it. Get anything and everything on your record!

This goes back to the minor inconvenience now for a big payoff later. If you go to the docs regularly when things aren't right, you could walk out of the military at any point, based on the severity of your claims, with a 100% disability rating. As of 2021, it is a **$3,100/month** check, tax-free, for the rest of your life!

Even if you don't listen to any of the financial inputs I laid out in the rest of this book, please, go to the damn doctor! Be a burden, be a squeaky wheel! It is for your benefit down the road! And even if you served for two to three years, talk to your Veterans Service Officer (VSO). I am almost 100% positive there is something you can claim! Rotating work schedules, separation from loved ones, PT, and marching make quite a bit of impact on the body and psyche!

Step 3: Plan Your Second Life

So, what do you want to do when you are out? Do you want to become a civilian in the military doing what you are doing now? Do you want to make a 180-degree shift with your career when you get out? Do you want to start a business so you can work for yourself when you hang up your uniform? There are so many different options that you can do—best decide with a couple of years left on your contract to do the necessary prerequisites. I would say a minimum of 3-5 years left .

There are many options that the military/government provides to help service members make that transition to their desired directions and fully explore those. Use your Tuition Assistance to get the certificate you need, and use the Skillbridge program to help you gain experience. Do anything you can to set yourself up properly.

I decided to go multiple ways during my separation. I was a weather guy in the service, but I'd had a passion for finance for a while (if you couldn't have guessed by my authoring this book). I made a 180-degree shift and decided to start a business helping military members with their finances! So, based on my personal experience, DO Skillbridge if it is offered, especially if you will make a complete shift. It allows you to explore your new career while still being paid by the military and gain real-world experience. And if you aren't a dirtbag, you may get a full-time offer coming out of it, win-win. Now, keep in mind that you may take a pay cut when switching to a new career path, so adjust your budget accordingly and think of doing side hustles to help support your way of life. I took about a 20% pay cut, so keep that in mind.

If you decide to go the business route alone or to complement your post-military career, I would find a mentor to assist you in that journey. If you can, I ALWAYS recommend you find someone that has walked that journey already and learn from them. It will help accelerate you because you won't have to pick your disgruntled ass out of pitfalls every time you fall into one. After all, your mentor can point them out before you stumble into them. A truly valuable thing!

If you stick with your current path that you are already on, you will have the easiest time out of all the other options as you most likely must wear a different hat. So, enjoy that simplicity! I have nothing more to say on that! Maybe find a military member in the new company to help you navigate the world of corporate America; it can be a crazy confusing place for a recent separatee/retiree.

Step 4: Treat Yo Self!

In the great words of Aziz Ansari in Parks and Rec, "Treat Yo Self!" The military is not an easy journey; it is demanding—physically and mentally challenging. But you made it! And I hope, better off because of it from where you started.

But when can you officially retire and live off your investments? There are a few steps that you need to figure out.

1. How much do you expect to get from your Military Pension and/or VA Disability per month?
   Example: $5,000 per month.

2. How much would you like to live off per month during retirement? How much additional is that above your pension/disability?
   Example: I want $8,000 per month in retirement, so I need **$3,000** a month from my investments.

3. Multiply that desired additional monthly amount by 12.
   Example: $3,000 x 12 = $36,000/year.

4. Divide that per year amount by .04 or 4%.
   Example: $36,000/.04 = $900,000.

Note: 4% is a safe amount to draw from your retirement/brokerage account annually in retirement. It is safe enough that if you have a downturn in the market and your accounts dip in value, you will not be hard-pressed to keep living and on an average year, your accounts will continue to grow.

5. $900,000 in the example is the amount that you need in your brokerage and/or IRAs to make your desired monthly "pay" in retirement.

If you want to make an additional $10,000 per month to take some fantastic vacations and live your best life, you will need $3M in your accounts.

Hint: If you can achieve your desired amount in your traditional brokerage account, you can retire before age 63. And then your IRAs will be a substantial additional bonus after 63! Score!

Now is your time—use it how you want to! Go out there, live your life, and love it because you truly deserve it! And again, I hope this book was your guiding light to get you to that point in your life. Fair winds and following seas!

Homework

What are your biggest takeaways from this chapter?

_____

_____

_____

_____

_____

What is your next step?

_____

_____

_____

Any final notes?

_____

_____

_____

_____

_____

_____

In Closing

I would like to take the time to thank you for joining me on this journey of brain vomiting all my financial background growth, failures, and successes that has made me who I am today.

I hope this book has fulfilled my goal of plugging the gaping financial education hole that exists in the Military. I hope by the end of this book, you have gained a clearer picture of the road ahead, have an accurate step-by-step roadmap of the journey, and have the utmost intestinal fortitude to take those first of many steps forward. I also hope this gives you the confidence to mentor those below you, as you climb up the ranks, in how to be successful with their own finances… because, that is our job!

And even if you did not connect with my book, some of you may not, that is A-OK. I hope that this book spurred you on to find your own financial knowledge that speaks to you. Do your research and find the one that speaks to you and your financial goals. If you do have any questions, in the next section, I have multiple ways for you to get in touch with me.

I leave you with these closing thoughts. Successful finance execution is not about being smart...it is about not being dumb. Just like most decisions in life, sometimes the smartest decision is just saying "No." If it is too good to be true, then "No." If something forces you to use more brain cells than you have, then "No." If you are using your Ego more than your Brain, then "No." And lastly, if it smells like shit, and tastes like shit...it is probably shit. No kink-shaming here... but "No."

Ok, enough hand-holding; it is your turn to figure out if you are going to shit or get off the pot! Are you going to take what you learned in this book and apply it; or is this going to go on your shelf to collect ungodly amounts of dust? Best of luck.

CYA!

Ian

How to Get More Help

I have already mentioned this a few times throughout my book: a book can carry only a small portion of any given topic. Unless you want to write a damn encyclopedia or write a trilogy, there are going to have to be other destinations for information. So here we are:

Financial Health & Budget Workbook: If you haven't already downloaded my free Financial Health & Budget Workbook, then I implore you to do so. This provides you with the best financial foundation to improve your finances now and well into the future. Visit go.giwealthmanual.com/workbook to get your copy—this is to thank you for purchasing my book and spending time with me. So, thank you again.

The Military Wealth Making Process (MWMP) Power-course: This is my flagship course that not only reinforces the material in this book, but also further expands upon winning investment strategies, conquering taxes, and preparing now for your post-military life! Enrolled students have access to my coaches and me for any roadblocks that they may face in their financial journey. But, I must warn you…this course is

NOT for everyone. However, the value you receive will make it worthwhile if you choose to take it on. You can learn more about the course at go.giwealthmanual.com/masterclass.

Tactical Investing Group: This is my monthly subscription investing huddle. Join me while we walk through companies and investments that I am analyzing or ones that you want me to analyze. Learning is best absorbed if you can watch how it is done, instead of just reading about it. This will consist of a weekly Zoom call where you can join me and other enrollees live to walk through how to uncover golden investments. Visit go.giwealthmanual.com/TIG to learn more about joining me live!

Acknowledgments

First and foremost, I need to thank the countless men and women I had the pleasure and honor of serving alongside. I hope by writing this book I can help strengthen the fighting force financially for many years to come. YOU are the reason why I wrote this book, so I could plug some educational gaps I personally experienced in the military, and continue to serve after my Active Duty career came to an end…just wearing a different hat.

I also want to take the time to thank my family and friends; without you, none of this would be possible. Your constant belief in me to go after and reach my dreams is the catalyst in my doing so. I will be forever grateful! And thank you Katelyn for being my sanity check on my material so that I am able to provide the utmost value to my readers!

Lastly, to my mentors along the way, thank you! To Phil Town for growing and reinforcing my financial mindset and know-how, and to Kiana Danial for showing me the way to be able to find my passion, put it into action, and reach the audience that I want to ultimately help for the rest of my life, a big thank you!

About the Author

Ian Bergstrom – Veteran, Entrepreneur, & Finance Nerd

Ian Bergstrom is the CEO and owner of GI Wealth, a company specializing in helping and teaching military members how to have full control over their financial lives and reach their ultimate goals!

Originally from the small, farming town of Spencer, Ohio, Ian branched out and was accepted into The Ohio State University Atmospheric Science program. Upon graduation, he not only graduated as a Meteorologist but was also a commissioned Butter Bar through ROTC. He was in the US Air Force for just over 10 years where he served as a Weather Officer, reaching the rank of Major before separating to explore other passions. He served six years in Tucson, AZ. He spent a further three years in Alaska working with the Army as a Staff Weather Officer (SWO)…also known as an Air Force Appreciation Tour, damn Army, all those drawings in the porta-potties, one year in South Korea and finally three years in Arkansas. During his time on Active Duty, Ian fell in love with personal finance, mainly driven by a sense of wanting to be better than the pack financially, but also because the military sucks at teaching personal finance...so he wanted to plug this hole...so to speak.

Ian received his MBA in Finance to further gain additional experience with money...which funnily enough, helped him in 0 ways to improve his own financial situation, but it did reinforce his nerdiness with finances. So, when he finally got out of the military, he pursued a job within the financial sector...which provided him additional ammunition to drive his true passion for helping other military members achieve success.

Post-separating from the Air Force, Ian settled outside of Washington DC, where he continues his career within the financial sector and continues to grow his business and brand to help so many other military members grow!

If you have any questions for Ian, would like to request any additional information, or would like to work together, please reach out to him at ian@giwealthmanual.com.

Bibliography

[1] Hanson, Melanie. "Average Student Loan Debt by Year." Education Data Initiative. Last Updated January 19, 2022. https://educationdata.org/average-student-loan-debt-by-year

[2] Koncz, Andrea. "Salary Trends Through Salary Survey: A Historical Perspective on Starting Salaries for New College Graduates." NACE. Last Updated August 02, 2016. https://www.naceweb.org/job-market/compensation/salary-trends-through-salary-survey-a-historical-perspective-on-starting-salaries-for-new-college-graduates/

[3] Office of Financial Readiness. "A Guide to the Uniformed Services Blended Retirement System." US Department of Defense. Assessed January 03, 2022. https://militarypay.defense.gov/Portals/3/Documents/BlendedRetirementDocuments/A%20Guide%20to%20the%20Uniformed%20Services%20BRS%20December%202017.pdf?ver=2017-12-18-140805-343

Bilello, Charlie. "How to Think About Home Price Appreciation. Compound." Last Updated July 09, 2020. https://compoundadvisors.com/2020/homes-castles-and-price-expectations

Ziraldo, Katie. "What is the Average Mortgage Payment? Rocket Mortgage." Last Updated July 14, 2022. https://www.rocketmortgage.com/learn/average-mortgage-payment

Fernando, Jason. "Margin." Investopedia. Last Updated July 09, 2022. https://www.investopedia.com/terms/m/margin.asp

Investopedia.com. "Stocks." Assessed 16 Feb 2022. https://www.investopedia.com/stocks-4427785

Hayes, Adam. "Mutual Fund." Investopedia. Last Updated June 28, 2022. https://www.investopedia.com/terms/m/mutualfund.asp

Chen, James. "Exchange-Traded Fund (ETF) Guide." Investopedia. Last Updated February 26, 2022. https://www.investopedia.com/terms/e/etf.asp

Pipis, George. "Candlestick Charts in R." R-Bloggers. Last Updated March 18, 2021. https://www.r-bloggers.com/2021/03/candlestick-charts-in-r/

Seth, Shobhit. "Market Capitalization." Investopedia. Last Updated April 07, 2022. https://www.investopedia.com/investing/market-capitalization-defined/

Town, Phil. "Rule #1: The Simple Strategy for Successful Investing in Only 15 Minutes a Week!" 1st ed., 196 to 215. Three Rivers Press, 2006.

www.ingramcontent.com/pod-product-compliance
Lightning Source LLC
Chambersburg PA
CBHW071642210326
41597CB00017B/2076